An Anthology by Breast Cancer
Survivors, Previvors, Thrivers, &
their Families

Curated & Edited by Joely A. Serino
Cover Art by Jenna Philpott

Copyright © 2022 Joely A. Serino

Front & back cover artwork by © Jenna Philpott
Digital images of the original painting have been
granted to the editor of this book for use but
all rights remain with the artist
Interior layout/formatting by Joely A. Serino

All rights reserved. No part of this book may be reproduced, stored, or
transmitted by any means- whether auditory, graphic, mechanical, or
electronic- without written permission of the authors, except in the
case of brief excerpts used in critical articles and reviews.
Unauthorized reproduction of any part of this work is illegal and
is punishable by law.

All submissions selected and edited by Joely A. Serino.
All of the material in this book is the original work of each individual
writer/artist. Each writer/artist in this book holds the rights to his/her
own work and granted permission for his/her work to be used and
included in this anthology.

This book is a work of nonfiction. Unless otherwise noted, the editor
makes no explicit guarantees as to the accuracy of the information
contained in this book.

Because of the dynamic nature of the Internet, any web addresses,
links, or social media references contained in this book may have
changed since publication and may no longer be valid. The views
expressed in this work are solely those of each individual author and
do not necessarily reflect the views of the editor, and the editor
hereby disclaims any responsibility for them.

Joely A. Serino

To all those that came before us
& to all those that will come after us,
this one's for you.

For Nalie, Monica, Megan B., Lara, MacKenzie,
Julie, Grace, Pamela, Rabecca G., Bree, Sarah, Christina,
Shayla, Erica, Joyce, Rebecca B., Danielle, Lisa Q., Natasha,
Ameera, Cristina, Lauren, Gael, Kate, Melissa, Lisa M.,
Jessica, Amber, Marla, Megan A., Holly, Lee, Tamara, Berny,
Margot, Meg, Mara, Sierra, Steph, Rachael, Linda,
Chinwe, Raelene, Kim, and so many more.

Table of Contents:

Chapter 2: Had

Chapter 3: To

Chapter 4: Be

Joely A. Serino

Preface...

No matter the season of life you're in, hearing the words, "You are positive for breast cancer," is a devastating blow to one's emotions, mental health, and physical wellbeing; the type of trauma you can't ever fathom recovering from. Once diagnosed, your mortality is ever-present, closely sneaking up on you when times get tough, retreating into the background when your strength is regained but always haunting your sleep, along with the stories of lost breast cancer patients that others insist you listen to when they call with condolences. But the initial shock and tear-stained pillowcases are short-lived and quickly ripped away, only to be replaced by medical jargon, anxiety-filled appointments, and a multitude of treatments, leaving many confused and wondering what could possibly happen next. There is little time to mourn the body you held so sacred.

In an attempt to hold onto the person outside of the breast cancer diagnosis, survivors, previvors, thrivers, and their families often turn toward writing and the arts. Stringing the right words together in a poem to express the isolation breast cancer has filled us with, capturing our "new" body on canvas with sweeping brush strokes to come to terms with the reality that looks back at us in the mirror after every shower, writing "Dear Cancer..." letters to release the accumulated anger in order to move on are all ways that we cope and live day-to-day with the worrisome thoughts of recurrence. By making art out of our trauma, we are reclaiming what is ours in the most cathartic of ways.

Throughout *We Had To Be: An Anthology by Breast Cancer Survivors, Previvors, Thrivers, & their Families*, you will find the writings and artwork inspired by the experiences felt during each person's breast cancer journey. Whether it be an essay that recounts when a patient lost her lovely hair due to chemotherapy, a blog post with beautiful drawings dedicated to all the women who supported the patient as she sojourned through her diagnosis, an essay by a man with breast cancer representing the 1%, or a poem by a survivor's niece articulating how her strength impacted the whole family, you will be able to relate to the written word and artwork within this anthology if you are a patient, a survivor, a previvor, or a thriver, and you'll get a glimpse into the mind of a breast cancer patient if you're looking for insight on how to support your loved one.

A Letter from the Editor...

On January 7th 2020, I sat in a cold office at the local hospital, holding my husband's hand a little too tightly because I knew. Call it a premonition, call it women's intuition, an omen, or a prophecy, I just had a bad feeling. The way she said my name, the gesture of her hand to chair, the fake smile plastered across her face to hide the sadness she had for me were like bright neon arrows all pointing to positive. Her reports did indeed indicate that the mass they found at my yearly gynecologist appointment was Invasive Ductal Carcinoma, a common type of breast cancer. The rest of that appointment was a shaky blur. I listened to her statistics and looked at her graphs, but all I could think about was that no one in my family had suffered from cancer, nevermind breast cancer, so how could this be? Aren't I too young to have breast cancer? What about my job? Could we afford all of this treatment on two teacher's salaries? Am I going to die? Like a classic pinball machine, the questions jumped from one to another in my inner monologue, and the only thing I heard the doctor say was, "...breast cancer." Once we were out of the hospital and in the parking lot, a folder full of information in hand and a cold chill stinging my tear-stained cheeks, I completely fell apart in my husband's arms, the first falling of many.

After that official diagnosis, things moved at lightning speed. My team drew up a plan, and within a week, I was having surgery. What no one knew was that a global pandemic was about to hit, and the epicenter was exactly where I live. In order to keep the patients safe at my cancer hospital, no visitors were allowed. Almost every appointment, scan, treatment, and surgery was done completely alone. There was no one to hold my hand while I sat scared to death in the chemotherapy chair, no one to hug me in the oncologist's office when I got bad news, and no one to guide me toward the positive when my glass was looking half empty while sitting in that hospital. Although my husband was always waiting for me with warm hugs in the parking lot, I was alone, experiencing each piece of the journey by myself, and I felt it in every sense of the word.

After two surgeries, six months of chemotherapy, six weeks of radiation, and a NED (No evidence of disease) stamped on my file, I had entered the most difficult phase of my cancer journey, what they call "Survivorship." For over a year, I went through the motions, completing every test, surgery, and treatment my doctor required without question. I was finally able to pick up my head, wiping the cobwebs away, just to question, "What the hell just happened to me?" How do I fit into this world that moved on without me? Who am I now, after going through such a difficult cancer experience all alone? Surely, I've changed! Will I still fit in at work, with my friends, with my family, and especially, will my husband recognize this new person that metamorphosed into a strong, outspoken, fierce woman? What saved me during my unique cancer experience, and while in the throws of survivorship, was writing poetry. I wrote everyday about the treatments that I had undergone, about the pain, about friends who seemed to abandon me and those that stepped up for me, about the new woman I was becoming. In the end, I had a small collection of poetry about the truths of breast cancer, the real breast cancer, without the pink frilly ribbons.

With these breast cancer poems in hand, I thought a lot about what I wanted to do with them. I could self-publish them on my own, creating a book solely about my breast cancer experience. However, after going through my entire cancer journey alone, and now suffering from Medical PTSD because of that, I didn't want to do anything alone that pertained to breast cancer ever again. After speaking to my writing mentor and others in my writing community that I have great respect for, I decided that creating an anthology, filled with stories, poems, blog posts, journal entries, letters, and artwork, would not only reveal how each person's breast cancer experience is different, but it would also show how our stories and feelings are similar, helping those in the middle of treatment feel not so alone. And metaphorically, this would be the first part of my breast cancer journey that I wouldn't have to do alone. My poems, describing the hardest thing I've ever had to do, would be surrounded by the writing and artwork of the amazing people in the breast cancer community. And that's how *We Had To Be* was born.

With the birth of this idea for a book, came a name that has special meaning as well. When someone is diagnosed with cancer and begins treatment, they are automatically labeled as a warrior, a fearless fighter, a courageous hero. In reality, we are just doing what our doctors tell us to do. We are going through the motions each day to stay alive, scared to death of what the future holds. We aren't doing anything special, and to receive a moniker like "warrior" is a lot to live up to. The pressure to be this fearless fighter for everyone who loves you can often be even more daunting than going through the treatments themselves. With that being said, we **had** to be fighters, we **had** to be fearless, and we **had** to be strong because we didn't have any other choice if we wanted to live.

Aside from reading, learning, and possibly relating to the numerous experiences from breast cancer patients and their families written within this book, the profits gained from your purchase of *We Had To Be* will be donated towards organizations that use 100% of their donations towards breast cancer research. I have seen too many metastatic breast cancer patients on social media, many who have become my close friends, have to say goodbye to their families and leave little children behind because of this horrific disease. If I could use my skills, writing and self-publishing, maybe I could make a small difference in the lives of those suffering from metastatic breast cancer by helping to fund research with the sales of this anthology. With that, thank you for your purchase.

While reading *We Had To Be*, I encourage you to do so with precaution for your own mental health and well-being. Some of the writings within this book are quite heavy and may be triggering to those who have experienced cancer firsthand. If you are feeling upset, angered, or especially saddened by any of the submissions, I encourage you to take breaks so as not to distress yourself further. Also, please be reminded that each submission expresses the thoughts, feelings, and views of each individual author and do not necessarily reflect my own personal opinion. I am simply the editor bringing these stories to light and giving a voice to the amazing people in the breast cancer community.

Before you begin, please know that there is no special way or order in which to read *We Had To Be* except with an open heart and empathy for the authors who have decided to share their writing and artwork with the world. If you or a family member have been diagnosed with breast cancer, are going through treatment, or are navigating your way through survivorship, please use this book as a reminder that you are not alone in your journey.

All my best,
Joely A. Serino

We Had To Be

WH2B: The Playlist

We had to be fearless. We had to be reliant. We had to be vulnerable. We had to be relentless. We had to be in debt. We had to be bald. We had to be warriors. We had to be knowledgeable. We had to be in pain. We had to be courageous. We had to be strong. We had to be sick. We had to be [we didn't have any other choice].

*Using your phone's camera or a QR Code Scanner, scan the QR Code below to get the WH2B Playlist, and listen along while you read for a full mixed media experience.

We Had To Be

Chapter 1:
We

Who are we, as people and as breast cancer patients?

"Cancer doesn't have a face
until it's yours or someone
you know."
-Anthony Del Monte

We Had To Be

I cried in a meeting today.
It's been almost a year
since my diagnosis,
But my breath still catches
in my throat when I have
to say the words,
"I have breast cancer,"
out loud.

-Joely A. Serino

Not a Pink Ribbon

I am not a pink ribbon.

I am not an initiative.

I am not a fundraiser.

I am not an October event.

I am a jagged mastectomy scar

that cuts across the left side

of my chest

every day of the year.

I am a cherry blossom tattoo

which thinly masks that scar,

beautiful and ugly and triumphant

all in one.

I am a survivor,

a thriver,

an Amazon warrior,

a mother, a wife, a daughter,

a sister, an aunt, a friend.

I am a novelist, a poet,

and a fighter,

always a fighter,

until my last breath.

I am incomplete,

missing one puzzle piece,

yet I am more than whole

because I am

still alive.

But

I am not a pink ribbon.

-Cathy Gigante-Brown

I Am Beautiful

Look past the pallor and the puff. Ignore the weird post-chemo fluff. If you look through the stubby eyelashes, beyond the dark sunken circles, you will see I am, like you are, spectacularly beautiful. Yes, I am. And this is why...

... because of the love that surrounds me, fills me up and shines back out into the world. I'm staggered by the love and kindness that has flowed my way during the last 6 months. At the beginning of this debacle, I knew there would be beauty, and this is it. The swirling blanket of human kindness that moves to hold people who need it. I've seen it come into action for others, and even been a part of it from the other side. But, to be the recipient is to know love. It's mind blowing, humbling, and exquisite. And as all of your love is reflected back out of my tired eyes, along with the gratitude and wonder of it, I am beautiful.

... because I'm middle aged (there I said it!) and a bit battered. I have 41 years of life, and nestled among the creaks, creases, scars, and broken bits is the beginnings of wisdom. There are stories and adventures. Lucky escapes, mistakes, and a lot of laughs. And the richness and depth of a life well lived is beautiful.

… because I'm a broken bowl. Who wants perfect? My good friend reminds me often of kintsugi, the Japanese art of fixing broken pottery with gold and silver. Broken things can be healed to be even more beautiful. My dressings came off today. A deep breath moment that you can't prepare for! But, New Shiny will heal to be more beautiful than before. If only the NHS filled surgery wounds with gold and silver!

… because I have kind green eyes that will not dim. I have a smile that will shine for anyone who needs it. And I've always rather liked my nose, although age is making it a little more witchy. I am also beautiful because I can love myself unconditionally, and this brings me peace. Peace and love, man, everyone knows they are beautiful, even without the acid!

… because I look like my mum and my sister. And they are very beautiful.

In this social media ridden world, perfection seems to own beauty. I think the broken, the crooked, and the real should reclaim her. Beauty is multifaceted, and by only sharing and receiving good times and filtered selves, we miss out on experiencing the full spectrum. And we lose our ability to see the beauty in ourselves when life isn't fit for Instagram. I am beautiful, and so are you. Everyday and in many ways.

-Louisa Trunks

She

She's a girl
She's a woman
She's a daughter
She's a sister
She's a friend
She's a mother

She's a warrior
With her army behind her
She has iron running through her veins
And hope running through her heart
She stared death in the face and
has the scars to prove it
She permeates strength in her beauty
She's a diamond that can't be broken
She lives every day of her life
She believes in herself
She inspires me and everyone around her
She's phenomenal
She's a cancervivor

-Sally Martin

Bionic Breast Warrior

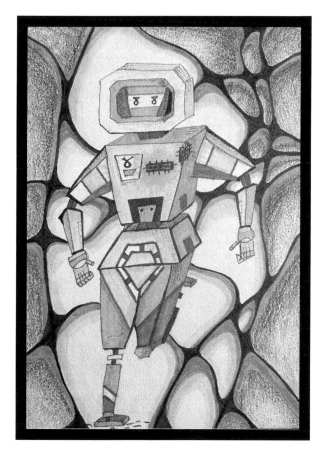

The Bionic Breast Warrior is aimed to show a woman's warrior-like journey through a breast cancer diagnosis, treatment, recovery, and coping with the future and fear of it returning. A tough outward armour bravely showing the patched up war wounds, but no one can see the real feelings and fragility inside.

-artwork and description by Kathryn Bassett

Magnetic Poetry

-Joely A. Serino

Who's There?

I stand and I stare,
Lip hair, grey hair, and wrinkles
Who's that in the mirror
Looking back at me.

I stand and I stare,
The eyes are familiar
Smile, gentle and kind,
It must be my Grandma,
Or even my mum.

I stand and I stare,
But, that's not my Grannie
Not even my mum
Is that the lady
I have become?

I stand and I stare,
But now I can see
Life lines, not wrinkles,
Hair silver, not grey,
All of a sudden I recognize me!

-poem & photography by
Diane Leopard

Alone

I cry heavy tears
in a room where
everyone sits

             alone.

Pods of comfortable chairs
set up 6 feet apart
that hold nothing but

             patients.

Just a sea of bald heads,
and shaky hands,
and bad news,
we're all there for
the same reason.

And I wish some stranger
would come over and hug me,
take my hands and ask

             "Is everything ok?"

So I can pour out my fears
onto their lap,
give someone else the weight
I've been carrying with me,
                    but they can't.
We are all dying in this room,
some faster than others,
and it's too risky to come within
6 feet of me.

So I hug myself,
squeezing my own shoulders,
consoling myself,
shadows waltzing close behind
on the walls surrounding me,
                    like family.

Anything to get through this day.
Anything to not feel so alone.

-Joely A. Serino

If I Didn't Fight

Had to inhale
My pride
Cut out the cancer
That was embedded
Deep inside

As tears run down my face
I'm still here in this place
Enjoying another taste
Days intertwined with black lace
Cheated fate
Destiny rewritten
Grim Reaper seems smitten

Every exhale a gift to me
Living each day happily
Earned because I fought
With all my might
Grasping at straws
That seemed out of sight

Positive mentality
Still remains
Overcoming dooming fatality
Though my life now
Never the same

I'll not wallow
Trying to put off my sorrow
Thinking about an impending task
Living now impulsively
I'll do me
There is no one I even have to ask

Ringing the bell
In the grave
I'm not ready yet
Had to be brave
Climbing out of the muddy trenches
That I was buried in
More time
I did win

Living in a world
That I created
Bittersweet memories
Of past once hated
Ripped off the disguise
Of the lingering lies
This took years of tries

I wouldn't be here today
If I didn't fight for my life
In my own way
This time is all mine

This is the atmosphere
I've always wanted
I'm giggling inside can't you hear
Even though past shadows stay near
So thankful that I made it
Scorched by the fire
But now I stay lit
Climbing on my scars
While reaching for the stars

-Gina Carrillo, Black Widow

Swamp/Sea

I float and I fall

With the waves

And the sludge

Or maybe it's just the sand

Beneath my feet

Moving

Flowing

But I cannot always stand

Just when I catch my footing

Another swell comes

And washes me away again.

-Kylee Cameron

The Elevator

There's a seat in the elevator,

because we are all dying a slow, arduous death here.

There's a seat in the elevator

just in case I'm there when it's my time to collapse,

For when my legs fold under me,

my arms too weak to hold myself up.

There's a seat in the elevator

because eventually the energy will be drained

from the holes they keep making in my arms,

and the passion for life will be absorbed by the poison

they keep pumping into me.

There's a seat in the elevator

for when I can't stand anymore.

-Joely A. Serino

 Pink World

Many folks don't even realize that men have mammary tissue let alone that they can get breast cancer. Although it is only 1% of the number of women who get breast cancer, for the men that get the diagnosis, it is devastating.

My diagnosis was a slow roll spanning almost three months from initial suspicions to final diagnosis. A slowdown in work meant I was able to go to the doctor to deal with some pending health issues. One of those issues was a lump in my left breast. I thought I knew what it meant. My mother had died of breast cancer, my brother had breast cancer ten years earlier, and my other brother prophylactically had his breast tissue removed because they were extremely sensitive. The family doctor pointed out that I also had a very small lump in my right breast. He gave me a referral to the local breast clinic telling me that I would get a call for some appointments in the next couple of days.

The first appointment call was for an ultrasound in a month. When the next call came it was for a mammogram the next day, if I could make it. I could and asked if they could fit the ultrasound in at the same time so I wouldn't have to take two days off of work. After the mammogram, the radiologist came and said they would get me to the ultrasound in a few minutes. Not a good sign. When the nurse called the next day to make the third appointment for biopsies, my breast cancer suspicions felt confirmed.

When I arrived for the appointment with the Breast Health Specialist, I was handed a clipboard and was asked to fill in some information. The first side was pretty straight forward. Allergies, medications, family history. It was when I turned the page over that I realized that I had entered what my brother calls "The Pink World." The entire waiting room erupted in stress relieving laughter when I read the first two questions out loud. "Was I still having periods?" and "Was I pregnant?" Not to minimize the fact that in Canada 25,000 women will be diagnosed with breast cancer and 5,000 will die this year, but there will be 220 men diagnosed as well, and 40 of them will die.

Seven days later when I was shown the biopsy results, things started to move very quickly. Both biopsies were Invasive Ductal Carcinoma, Estrogen positive, Progesterone positive, and HER2 negative. The concern was - has the cancer spread? A most amazing Navigator Nurse organized blood work, a CT scan, and a bone scan. These tests took up the rest of my day.

Despite the quick work when I met with the surgeon the next morning, we still didn't have a definitive answer to that question. While the preliminary bone scan showed nothing (good news), the CT scan showed a large mass in my right lung (middle lobe - about five cm across). We needed to figure out what it was. It might be as simple as scarring from my go-round with tuberculosis when I was in Panama, it could be a third primary site for a completely unrelated cancer, or it could be metastasized breast cancer. I was scheduled for a fine wire lung biopsy in the near future (sometime in the next two weeks).

The fine wire biopsy wasn't happening fast enough, so the team decided to aim for an ultrasound guided endoscopic biopsy. Further testing determined that it was NSCLC, non-small cell lung cancer. A PET scan confirmed that it was in some lymph nodes between the lungs as well as some small spots in the left lung, staging it at IIIC.

The breast cancer receded into the background at this point with the priority being treatment of the lung and lymph tumors. The oncologists took a curative approach with aggressive chemo/radiation of the tumors. Six cycles of paclitaxol/carboplatin over six weeks with concurrent thirty days of radiation. "The first two weeks will be a breeze. By the third week you'll start to feel some effects. And the final two weeks will leave you on the ropes," said the chemo nurse. True that.

I took six weeks to recover and then had a double mastectomy for my breast cancer. Four days after that, I started on the recently approved immunotherapy drug

Durvalumab. I also started Tamoxifen for the breast cancer. After fourteen of a planned twenty four treatments, a CT scan revealed that the tumors in my left lung had begun to increase in size. This time a fine needle biopsy was done to determine whether these were metastasized breast cancer or lung cancer. When it was confirmed that these were indeed lung cancer, my lung cancer was restaged to IV, and I started treatment with Afatinib. This targeted therapy was incompatible with Tamoxifen, so I stopped that.

Four years later, physically I feel fine. I run 5K three times a week. Emotionally it has been a bit of a roller coaster. In some ways I'm feeling fatalistic about it. "It is what it is." Mentally, I'm a curious fellow, so my days are filled with advocacy. I recently completed the STARS program, a training program for lung cancer patient research advocates. Spiritually, as my late wife said, "Angus, you are just a rock." I don't know what God has for me in all of this. I have a sense that they aren't finished with me yet.

-Angus Pratt

The scars on my skin hurt the least...

The inside of my eyelids

are collages of a life that

I can't relate to,

        Barely remember,

                Can't recognize.

They aren't memories,

they are stains:

        Red wine on white silk,

                Blood on white linen.

I scrub tirelessly at indelible stains,

        slices on skin,

            self-inflicted secret thoughts,

But it's no use.

        I mourn over their permanence.

My skin is a roadmap,

a blueprint to the cloudy trauma

that plagues my unconscious.

I trace each scar with gnawed at

bloody fingertips,

willing myself to accept each new blemish,

longing to embrace a me I don't yet understand.

-Joely A. Serino

I'm Not Ready to be a Memory

I'm not ready to be a memory

But we all will be

Someday

And when I am, I hope
That you will remember
That
I tried to figure things out
I made questionable choices
but did learn how to make better ones
The hard way
When I knew better, I did better
Always the hard way

I hope that you saw me as someone
with open eyes, ears, and heart
I was not for everyone
But I was real with all the ones
Who mattered

Real funny
Really good at recommending binge-worthy shows and
books
Real good at smelling good
A real good hugger

A mother who wanted to be a real good mom
A spouse who tried to do better
Real good at trying
A real good friend

I hope that you will remember my words
And that they meant something
I hope they take me places
Some of them with you

-Kate Ellis

She

She was always special to me. She was the big sister I never had, my first best friend. She was beautiful and didn't even know it. She taught me to be strong and have a backbone. I wanted to be just like her. If she liked something, I had to like it too. She never let anything defeat her or take her down.

Even when she was diagnosed with breast cancer and things kept getting harder, she kept going. Covid spiked, treatments got harder and more frequent, surgeries were postponed, test results were delayed. The waiting period was enough to make you mad.

BUT NOT HER. She kept going, she kept working, she kept fighting, she kept smiling. She did it with positivity. She was thriving just trying to survive.

She was meant to win the battle her father lost.

-S.A. Lucero

Cancerversary

I let my thoughts wander

into the crevices of my mind,

thinking back to this time last year.

365 days ago, I went about my day carelessly,

all smiles.

Fingers snapping and hips swaying,

as we danced together in the kitchen

to our favorite songs.

52 weeks ago, I thrived,

with a "that could never happen to me" mentality,

invincible to the stories we hear

by sad souls at the neighborhood bar.

1 year ago, I thought I was done growing;

I knew my innermost woman,

and no one could change her.

So naive, I was.

That was all short-lived and fleeting.

Cancer changes everything about who you are,

how you exist and evolve,

and what it means to truly live life.

-Joely A. Serino

December 2020

"Trauma transformed into present strength…"-Ebony Kennedy
The Story of Me by the doll who sits on my bookshelf
I come from a long line of women
Women who have survived
Who have bled and wept and healed and recovered.
We are warriors who have fought off demons, tangled
with angels cloaked as devils, given birth to new life,
and fed babes suckled to our breasts
The very breasts that were cut off
Cut away
Swollen with pestilence
Sliced
Crudely stitched and sliced again
I emerged to bare my scars proudly,
But the insides of me still hurt and weep for who I once was.

The slope and curve of my beauty,
the abundance of my blossom,
The pleasure I once gave, gone.
All left.
>Gone
>Destroyed
>What is left of me?

I am more than my scars and even more than the parts yet to mend.

I am Hope.
I am Blessing.
I am Warrior. Survivor.
And I speak for all those not yet ready.
For those to come after, to offer company and solace.

TO BE REAL
I AM A REAL WOMAN
I breathe life in the one that builds life again.

My name is Una.

I am the Origin.

- Stephanie Burlington Daniels

She, me, we - all three.
And my daughter? ...Maybe

-quote & artwork by Kristina Smith

The First Five Days of Cancer

Five years have passed since cancer last stopped by. During that time, I didn't dare to dwell on the possibility that it would return again so soon. But here it was, confirmed by a biopsy. Cancer was back in my life. Would things be different this time? Previously, I was a caregiver. How would I handle myself this time as the patient?

My young daughter has already reached double digits. She shows no evidence of disease and thrives on stages, sports fields, and in classrooms. To her, cancer is a distant memory. As her caregiver, by her side through a four year battle, the memory is more intact. It is ingrained in my being, if you will. Because of my daughter's example, I know I will get through this. She's my reason to remain in a positive mind frame. I'm so thankful that she set that standard.

Time stopped the moment I heard the words, "I'm sorry, it's cancer," for the second time. A deep anguish rushed over me. I was so sad for my four kids and husband. It would be exhausting for us to deal with cancer again, twice in such a short time span. As we entered the surreal, gray area that separated us from 'life without cancer' and placed us at the starting line of another grueling marathon, a persistent question repeated itself over and over again. "Why? Why, Cancer?" I wished one visit had been enough.

We were very public during my daughter's battle. We welcomed anyone who wanted to be there and support us. We ran 5Ks, held fundraisers, attended events, and the energy lifted us up. My daughter and our family felt an intense love and devotion that we had never experienced before. This time, I felt more private and reflective. My husband of twenty years was the only other soul who knew of my diagnosis, and we decided to take this intermission to catch our breath. There would be a five day pause before we would know the stage, prognosis, protocol, and my survival statistics.

During those first five days of cancer, I would experience excruciating fear, debilitating panic, along with sobbing sessions that concluded in epiphanies. I decided to let go and remain open to what would come.

Day 1

The first day was a Monday. My husband and I cried on and off the entire day. We decided not to tell our children right away. There were so many unknowns. We were not calm. Our kids were young—all four were under fourteen years old. Cancer wasn't a new word in their vocabulary, still, we weren't ready to reintroduce the concept. The ride home from school pickup was particularly hard. "Why is Mommy so sad?" my five year old asked.

That night, I mentally conducted a body scan and began to acknowledge the odd pains that had lingered over the past six months, as well as the fatigue I'd been feeling. I promised my husband I would be a good patient. "I will never leave your side," he responded and canceled the first business trip he had scheduled since the COVID-19 pandemic had shut down the world.

Day 2

On Tuesday, the second day, there were less tears and hopelessness. A rush of energy coursed through me. I joined a Facebook group of newly diagnosed patients and filled an Amazon cart with hundreds of dollars worth of items that were recommended on past threads. I probably would not need or buy the items, but I felt productive. I found a used recliner on a Buy Nothing group after discovering that it would be easier to recover and sleep upright after surgery. That night, I was awake researching until three in the morning.

"This will be hard," my husband said. "Don't get mad at me," he pleaded, hoping my stress would not land on him. He mentioned that he felt as fatigued as I did. "We are connected," I said. "I'm sure that's why we're feeling exactly the same way."

Day 3

On Wednesday, I realized that I needed a project—something to focus on other than cancer. I needed a reason to move forward, to get beyond cancer. I wanted an alternate goal, something other than just surviving. "You know me, I need to multitask," I said to my husband. He took my lead, he dreamt with me, and we began to plan. An idea began to take shape. We would purchase a plot of land and build a barn together as a family. There would be animals, rainwater collection, and wind power. Our goal would be self-sufficiency. The project would bring comfort to our family and become an escape, free of devices and drama. It would be our legacy, built with love and hope. Built from the ashes of cancer. We cried all over again.

Day 4

On Thursday, I decided to stop chaotically researching. There were countless rabbit holes and many of the posts and articles that I found online focused only on what could go wrong with treatment and surgery. I wondered if those who had positive outcomes didn't take the time and trouble to post about it. Maybe they were superstitious or maybe they were too busy living. Everything went well, so they had moved on and no longer returned to the forums. I could understand that. I promised myself to pay it forward and give hope to others when I got through this.

I also decided that I would apply a time limit on how long I spent researching online every day. When I hit that limit, I was finished for the day. Ultimately, I would put trust in my medical team. Even though I was still terrified to the core, the endless searching only seemed to amplify my anxiety.

Day 5

On day five, a sunny, cloudless Friday, I was inspired to plan a hike for our family. We needed the exercise and something physical that we could do together. I found a nature preserve with a cave system about an hour away that we had never visited.

On the hike, step by step, I imagined myself returning to health. Nothing else mattered but restoring my health and celebrating at this same cavern, sometime in the future. As we walked, my phone pinged with an email notification. The subject line read, "Results available." My heart started racing. I suspected it was the pathology report from my biopsy. The results had been emailed over before the doctor was available to speak with me.

I realized that I could open the email and try to interpret everything in the report on my own. No, I decided. I wanted it explained to me in person. I would have this one last weekend, suspended in limbo, but with a clear mind, an acute awareness, and an open heart.

After the weekend, I would hear from my medical team. Whether I was metastatic or at an earlier stage, I knew that I'd take the opportunity to fight. There was no other choice. I was hurtling towards a journey that would require me to go inside of myself again and find superhuman strength.

I planned to stand my ground during the upcoming battle. On the other side, I would join my daughter and call myself a "survivor," just like she does. This time, I felt just as vulnerable, but I was also more prepared, more introspective, and more accepting. Challenges are a part of life. I was ready to carry on, to get to the other side of it. Let's do this. Sayonara cancer.

-Sky Khan

Hearts in the Sand

In her pale pink chiffon gown,

a flower wreath in her freshly done hair,

curly soft tendrils framing her sweet face,

she walked down the shell trimmed aisle toward her hero.

Not her first love;

Experience and time took that away from her long ago.

But her eternal love, her everlasting love, her last love.

And as he watched her, one could tell he was so proud of her.

Not because of her accomplishments,

or degrees,

or her fancy job,

but because she made it there.

She pulled through.

She walked down the aisle by herself

and that was an accomplishment all on its own.

And I got to witness it.

One of only five guests present

because yesterday she wasn't feeling well,

yesterday she got sick at the pool,

yesterday, while we were drinking pina coladas at the pool bar,

she couldn't keep her lunch down.

So we jumped up and grabbed a towel.

"Oh my goodness! Are you okay?"

"This sun is deadly! You have to be careful out here!"

"Did you eat something today, dear?"

And that's when we found out that she had breast cancer,

that it had traveled to her brain,

that the cancer cells were floating throughout her spinal fluid,

and she didn't have much time left,

that they were in love,

and they ran away together to get married before it was too late,

that maybe, just maybe, she could get on his great insurance,

and they could find a cure,

and him being a pilot, they could fly into the sunset,

and live happily ever after.

So we talked by the pool while I held a cool towel on the back of her neck,

and the guys got us bottles of water.

We bonded over the meds we take for our nausea;

while I didn't have cancer, I suffer from a stomach ailment,

and we arranged to have dinner that night,

where we shared drinks and laughed,

and I helped her to the bathroom,

because she suddenly was losing her balance and had trouble walking.

And that's when they invited us to their wedding the next day.

"We want you to come," he said.

"We wouldn't have it any other way," she added.

"It feels like fate," he cajoled.

And we weren't sure if it was too many drinks,

the tropical breeze,

or something written in the Dominican stars,

but at 2:00 p.m. the next day,

we decided to walk down the beach to see them tie the knot.

It was our anniversary after all;

how romantic would it be to relive the moment at someone else's

wedding?

And there they were,

just the two of them and the officiant.

It couldn't have been more perfect.

I was her and she was me in that moment.

There was no disease, no worries, just love.

We saw the two of them here and there

during the rest of our anniversary vacation.

She continued to worsen throughout the trip,

not being able to walk or keep a meal down.

We exchanged information before they went back to Chicago,

and we learned that only two months after their wedding,

she passed away.

One year later we went back to that same beach in Dominican

Republic,

and at 2 p.m. on August 14th,

using a stray piece of driftwood,

I drew two hearts in the sand with their initials in it,

to commemorate the miracle of love we witnessed that day,

because that was their beach,

would always be their beach.

No matter how many footsteps traipse across it,

no matter how many couples unite in that same spot,

on that same date,

as far as I'm concerned, that place belongs to them.

This year when I was diagnosed with breast cancer,

I thought a lot about her,

how hard it must've been to put on that pale pink chiffon gown,

that flower crown in her freshly curled hair that framed her sweet

face,

to smile through it all while she ached.

I know that ache now,

the inability to walk and keep a meal down.

And while on that day she was me,

I ask myself today,

am I her?

-Joely A. Serino

Cancer During the Holidays

Having cancer during the holidays is hard.

It's hard to feel thankful on Thanksgiving when you don't have your health to be thankful for,

When you look in the mirror and don't recognize yourself,

When, even after chemo is done, your eyelashes and eyebrows are still falling out and your body aches like you're 85 years old.

It's hard to feel the joy, as you light the menorah for Hanukkah, when inside there is so little joy to be found,

When all you feel is pain, sadness, anger, and fear for all you have gone through and still have to go through,

When you're grieving the last few weeks with your body as you know it, before you'll lose part of yourself, changed forever.

I'm trying my best to fight on,

But it's so hard.

-Stacy Meisel

Warrior

They say that I'm a warrior now,

A part of some elite club,

My initiation the strands that

lay on my bathroom floor.

                        But I'm no hero.

                        I'm no warrior.

The only battle I've fought

is the one against the coward

that is currently squatting the available

space in my head,

I willingly lay on my sword

at least two times a day,

My lips stumble across the

beautiful words I

befriended long ago,

And fat tears fall heavy

with reflections of memories

lining the path to my recovery,

filling my airways,

drowning me in my sleep,

a suffocation of screams

jolting me awake.

Tell me, when will the nightmares stop?

Tell me the nightmares will stop.

-Joely A. Serino

We Had To Be

Chapter 2:
Had

All the things you had to do, had to endure, had to change to save your own life...

"The only person who can save you is you; That was going to be the thing that informed the rest of my life."
-Sheryl Crow

We Had To Be

She Had to Be Her Own Hero

She had to find the strength she never knew she had
She had to have faith far bigger than her fears
She had to learn it's okay to let your guard down and cry
She had to let go of her comfort and her thick beautiful hair
She had to be stripped of all her feminine features to realize
that those features don't make you beautiful
She had to feel the sunlight hit her soul and create a fire
within
She had to armor up for battle each day because this war was
neverending
She had to keep going, even when she felt defeated
She had to cry herself to sleep because she was afraid of the
unknown
She had to fight for her life and her will to live
She did all this, not knowing how her strength and will to fight
would impact others
She did all this with a smile on her face, hiding all the tears
and pain
She did all this because...
She had to be her own hero.

*Dedicated to Auntie Loly, a breast cancer warrior,
by S.A. Lucero

I've Never Had Beautiful Hair

I've never had beautiful hair.
I've never had those long, golden locks cascading down my figure,
Covering my gentle femininity in all the right places.
As a little girl, I thought I was gifted with this beauty,
my strawberry blonde curls swirling at the nape of my neck,
but it didn't work out that way.
So I always envied the girls that lined fashion magazines and runways,
their long blonde hair swishing behind them.

I've never had beautiful hair.
I've never had the exotic, silken, dark hair that hangs
 straight down the back,
swinging at the waist,
bangs highlighting mysterious eyes.
I was always quietly jealous of my Latina friends growing up;
those dark eyed, dark-haired beauties that made all the boys
drool and all the girls green-eyed.

I've never had beautiful hair.
I've never had the ginger-red curly tendrils that I always
wanted,
framing my face,
cupping my shoulders,
matching the tiny freckles that lay spotted across my nose
at the break of every summer.
No amount of hair dye could get me that natural ginger glow
that I dreamed of since meeting my 3rd grade teacher,
her hair, a natural, thick, burnt-orange that I adored all these
years.

But losing my hair to chemotherapy has taught me a lot about
hair.
As my husband patiently and delicately shaved my head,
tears falling to the bathroom floor
along with the clumps of hair I clung onto
until the last possible minute,
I finally realized,
slowly over time,
that I am so much more than my hair.

So I've never had beautiful hair, but I've always been smart.
Although I pushed myself to the limit,
my parents providing me with the best education money could
buy,
my father taught me that street smarts are just as important as
book smarts,
and that I could get anywhere in life if I could string the right
words together and stand up for myself.
And I don't need hair for that.

I've never had beautiful hair, but I've always been kind.
My grandma showed me that if someone asks for help,
you should never deny them,
as she donated to the 20+ churches and charities that asked for
"Just 25 cents a day."
And my students would tell you the same of me;
anything that is mine is theirs, if they asked,
including my time, my money, and my love.
And I don't need hair for that.

I've never had beautiful hair, but I've always been a creative.

Popsicle sticks, pipe cleaners, and drawing paper were my toys of choice,

my mom never denying me these "toys" for something new or popular.

And my love for art only grew from there.

Matching words with art in a blackout poem

and stringing sentences together to express myself

are the breath that fills my being.

And I don't need hair for that.

I've never had beautiful hair, but I've always been loyal.

My Italian upbringing taught me that when shown loyalty, you give loyalty, even to a fault.

And like a dog to it's owner,

the loyalty I have for my friends and family is fierce.

It's in my bones and ingrained in my DNA.

And I don't need hair for that.

And so cancer has changed my mind about hair;

what it used to mean versus what it means to me today.

While it encompasses our most prominent feature

and defines beauty for so many,

we are so much more than our hair.

-Joely A. Serino

Just One More

Just one more
I mutter as I shuffle
around the house,
that's become my haven,
my hideaway from this
hideousness that has
sabotaged my life

One more cannula
One more cold cap
One more dose of pre-meds
One more red devil chemo
One more handful of hair
One more week of nausea
One more week of injections
One more week of aching bones
One more week of nosebleeds
One more box of tissues
One more week of hell
Just one more
I can do this

-Sally Martin

Mirror

Each day when I look in the mirror
I see less and less of me.
It is as though my face is melting,
as I lose more of my eyebrows,
and my eyelashes,
which used to be thick
as paintbrushes.

Each day when I look in the mirror,
I search for something familiar
but it is fading, *I* am fading
as I somehow become larger,
moon-faced, mongoloid from the steroids,
and mysteriously, more becomes less.

Each day when I look in the mirror,
I seek pieces of me.
I know I'm in there somewhere,
broken, rearranged, hidden
but not whole.

-Cathy Gigante-Brown

Losing my beautiful hair-blocking the shower a year on! The indignity of it...

At the risk of sounding arrogant...nah fuck it...my hair was awesome! If I walked into a room, pretty much, I would have the nicest hair in there. It's not that I'm particularly competitive; it's just that I'm a pretty average woman, happily, but my hair was my defining feature. If a stranger was to describe me, this would be a good way to do it, "The one with the hair." It was very long, down to my waist, mega thick and wavy. It was my crowning glory and my comfort blanket. I was a terrible hair fiddler, and I am unapologetic about that. Being told I had to have chemotherapy that would make my defining feature, my hair, fall out was all my horrors at once. I'd look like a cancer patient; I wouldn't look like me. Cue identity crisis. I mean, I am more than the sum of a bunch of hair, but visual identity is so wrapped up with self-confidence. How was I going to cope with this less than subtle dissonance? I also have a scar on my head (from falling down the stairs trying to help a drunk ex-boyfriend), which I hate, so that was something I was struggling with too. The 'helpful' breast nurse suggested I draw a face on it. I silently wept, veiling the world out with my luxurious locks, whilst she twittered about some irrelevant shite. I also changed nurses after that!

I have two bags of my hair in the dresser in our dining room: one from when I was an easily influenced teen, being teased by the older girls about my hippy hair. Desperate to have my long hair cut off and fit in, I nagged on and on. Mum caved and took me in the end. I cried that night as I held my two long plaits. My Aunty and Grandmother had a plait each. They kept them all those years, until they were returned to me after they both died.

The other bag holds my pre chemo hair. My old school friend cut it shorter for me. It was an emotional night; I was terrified. She was upset, but she gave me a beautiful bob. I hated it, of course, but it was still my hair, and I loved that she did that for me. A song that stuck with me through this part was

"Hairdresser on Fire" by The Smiths:

"Can you squeeze me
Into an empty page of your diary
And psychologically save me
I've got faith in you
I sense the power
Within the fingers

Within an hour the power
Could totally destroy me
(Or, it could save my life)"

These lyrics spoke to me with a dual meaning, ringing true regarding both chemo and hair loss.

After a failed and very upsetting wig debacle, I decided quickly I would try the scalp cooling cap when having chemo instead. This is a cold cap device that actually freezes your head down to between -26 and -40 degrees C. Scientifically it slows down the cellular activity and blood flow to your scalp, so it stops much of the chemotherapy meds from reaching your hair follicles, theoretically. It hurts, but I found it bearable as it gave me something to focus on rather than the brutal drug regime. I was also wrecked on Lorazepam and snuggled in hot water bottles every time I had to wear it. First to go was my pubic hair, then bang on time (as estimated by the nurses), 17 days after chemo 1, my hair started to come out in handfuls. It's a really alarming thing to happen, but plucking it out does become strangely addictive. I was terrified to wash it, so for the first and only time in my life, I used a shower cap. I mastered the comb over and used a dark root spray to cover the patches where my scalp was visible. Did you know your scalp feels like a baby's head? It's such an odd feeling after years of having so much hair! I still lost around 80% of my hair, and my best friend Annabel shaved it off on the 19th of December 2018, in the bathroom of her house the night before my last chemo.

My two best friends Annabel and Noreen were my chemo girls, my sisters, and my rocks. Annabel cried as she shaved my hair off using her husband's clippers. We saved what little there was and put it into a box. The three of us had a pact that when my hair got too bad, they'd say, and we'd shave it off. The time had come. I looked like Friar Tuck with extreme alopecia. I was a sorry, sorry sight, especially considering, not 4 months ago, I had the most glorious mane. I felt numb and naked losing these sorrowful wisps, the last part of old me was gone, lying in a cold bathroom sink to be washed into the drain. Oh the metaphor!

My psychologist once referred to me as the keeper of the hair; how right she was! A year later, the shower drain still gets blocked. I'm sure, despite numerous flushes with caustic soda, it's my beautiful hair's legacy clogging up those pipes.

After finishing chemo, the final insult was that my remaining, yet sparse, lashes and brows dropped out. I thought I'd gotten away with it. How wrong I was, and who the hell was that really sick, broken looking woman looking back at me from the mirror? Seriously! I was vain and ok with that, but this took the piss!

-Amabel Mortimer

Bad News

It hits like a bolt

Out of the blue

Cuts a swathe through the life

You thought you knew

Dreams and futures torn asunder

All you can do is hang on

Fear and anger pulling you under

Waiting for, dreading, the day they're gone

Links to the past severed forever

While the world tells you to move on

Living seems like a painful endeavor

Still an inner voice says, "Stay strong".

One foot in front of the other, you keep going

You think you know what's to come

Praying for a miracle solution

But, sometimes, nothing can be done

Carry on, live your best life, to the fullest

That's how the game of life is won.

-Sarah Fawcett

Tending the Garden

They tell me this blossom
needs to be cut off the stem,
pinched back is the term
my gardener friends use.
It's good for the plant
to remove the more senior
flowers, those that are
weakening, fading, to allow
for new growth, new flowering.
But this hard cutting back
the doctors propose is meant
to prevent new growth,
not to promote it. The weeding,
the medical pruning, will be
absolute and I will carry on
with one less flower in my garden.
But today, I am still in full bloom.
A garden unto myself.

-Laura L. Hansen

Witch

A powerful potion

Brewing

Don't touch, or it will burn

Skin and flesh

The right ingredients

Are perfectly toxic

A poison, like an apple

Administered to kill

The thing that does the killing.

-A commentary on chemo

by Kylee Cameron

Castaway

I never expected to find myself

Castaway

At the beach.

But there I was -marooned by sorrow.

Isolated by grief.

I watched the crashing waves retreat.

And the roar of the ocean

Became a whisper.

Alone on the island

I found a way to be.

It was small steps.

First one then the other,

Leaving footprints in the sand.

Marking my SOS.

I became my own shelter

I hunted; made a fire.

I survived.

Darkness came

And the night sky filled with stars

But I felt their light upon me; And I knew.

Morning broke,

And the sun became a ball of fire,

High in the sky

Where there are no shadows.

And the ocean continued to whisper

And the gulls circled in the air.

I had never been alone on the island

When I found myself there.

-Fiona Lochhead

Humour

I **had** felt awkward when I expressed my plight,

I **had** to keep these moments distractingly light.

I **had** to cover up intrusive thoughts during each long, dark night.

Where my deepest fears would take hold and viciously bite.

I **had** comically expressed each twisted delight.

I **had** recalled stories that brought some light-

relief to my daughter - hand holding tight.

Strangely, my actions felt somewhat contrite.

I **had** used my humour, to mutate that evil tumour,

 from black into white, impending into slight.

I **had** to lessen my fright - her fright -

that was foremost in our sight.

I **had** jokingly 'named' my breast operations,

Dolly Part-one and Dolly Part-two.

The paradox that "One breast is saggy, the other is blue!"

I **had** sketched and placed a cartoon image in her view,

 of me face down in the MRI, with my boobs dangling through!

I **had** many stories of post-op lows, despite

- unbelievably singing 'Spongebob Squarepants',

whilst as high as a kite!

I **had** to keep life, deceivingly bright.

I **had** to choose between FIGHT or flight.

I **had** to fight, fight, fight,

 For the positive thoughts that this C-bomb might,

Just turn out alright...

It **HAD** to...right?

-Kathryn Bassett

The Illusion of Longevity, Shattered

"What's that lump?" my husband casually enquired, as he nestled in for a cuddle. And just like that he saved my life.

I didn't know it then, for some reason I was really nonchalant about the large lump. Isn't it funny how so often you can't see the big moments in life as they happen? They rarely have soundtracks or fanfares. They just slide in, and one moment that could have glided past like all the others, turned out to be the most crucial of my life.

My doctor checked my lump and calmly arranged an urgent appointment at the breast clinic. I still wasn't worried.

Thirslestaine Breast Centre is fabulous: A gorgeous Georgian building with smart facilities and some very kind inhabitants. It's filled with lots of women: those that are there for scans looking worried and a little bored, and those that simultaneously emanate 'strength' and 'broken.' They are the ones who are on the other side of the scans. They have seen death's face, and it shows. I sat there with enormous respect and empathy for each of them, but I still wasn't worried.

Dr. Sharma copped a feel and drew all over my boob; I think I cracked a few jokes. The Mammogramist squished them flat, took some pics. She told me I needed to go to the ultrasound room and took great lengths to explain that this was normal. Well, of course, why wouldn't it be? I lay on the ultrasound bed praising them for their warm jelly, and I hadn't once considered that it could be anything sinister.

"It does seem like a lump, I'm afraid."

Fuck! That's not what they would say if it was ok. And then I saw that she was looking at something else.

"What's that?" I spat, choking on the words.

"Your lymph, it looks like there is something in it." BOOM! Why is there no stronger word than 'fuck?' It just didn't cut it.

I was propelled into outer space. Made infinitesimal, and at the same time aware of the news being expandingly large. My brain went very busy and very quiet. They started to biopsy me, the spring loaded mechanism clanking loudly. They asked all the time if I minded them doing this and that to me.

"Ha! That's funny," I thought, "as if anything matters now."

A specialist nurse came in to take me to another room. I faltered, and three women caught me.

In the room, which was tiny and windowless, the nurse took my hands:
"I need you to know that we are really good at this, it's not all over. There is a lot we can do," she said, emphatically, with so much kindness. I was on my own as this was never supposed to be a thing, so I called my husband, Lee.

"Can you come?"

Obviously, he knew, but I still had to tell him.

"It's cancer." He crumpled inwards like a sucked in paper bag.

I asked Dr. Sharma whether there was any chance it wasn't. She told me that we never know for sure until the biopsy results.

There are no jokes now.

Her eyes told me the truth. This was unequivocally cancer, and the best I could hope for was that it hadn't spread. I could not think of my children without gut wrenching, soul squirming agony. They did not deserve this.

I had spent 10 years affecting everything possible in my universe to keep them as safe as I could, and I was going to be the one to hurt them beyond measure.

Somehow, we went home.

What do you do after D-Day (diagnosis day, for those whose brain is addled with babies/chemo/age/shit genes!)? How do you go on?

Lee and I did yoga at home. We went through the motions with tears streaming. Unsure what else to do. Reaching out to touch each other between poses.

I gazed at my sleeping children, reeling at all the things I would miss if this thing had gone terminal.

I went to so many scans and appointments; letter after letter dropping on the mat from Gloucestershire hospitals.

I sat at my desk and tried to work. Nothing. Brain freeze.

I walked round the supermarket looking at old people, really fucking angry at them. One guy in the world food aisle was shuffling along with his miserable old jowls. Moping. Why wasn't he skipping? Didn't he know how lucky he was to be old? I was 41. He had doubled that. Bastard. He's lucky I didn't poke him into the bombay mix.

I looked in the mirror and repeated 'cancer, cancer, cancer.' Nope! It's not my word; this isn't supposed to be.

I wrote this to my mum when she asked how I was: "I can see that if it's not terminal it will be THE strongest experience of my life, and that it will probably come to be some kind of blessing. The illusion of longevity has been well and truly shattered. It's like a veil has been lifted. Sort of like when you have a baby and a whole new part of reality is opened up to you. But for now, it's just about holding my head together until I know if it has spread. I can do shit times; there is beauty in them. But I really don't want to do death... yet.

I'm totally exhausted without being sleepy, shaken, clearly in shock and have all the physical manifestations of grief. But I'm actually doing pretty well all things considered."

A more British Brit would have said, "Fine."

I walked. The only time I felt like things might be ok was when I was on the hill.

I went like a zombie around secondary schools, trying to make decisions for my son about his future. The one that I might not be a part of.

And I spent hours yearning for 'home.' I sat in my house, looking at my family, feeling like I would never be able to go home again.

Eventually, after two very long weeks it was time to meet my surgeon. He strode in, shook my hand, looked me in the eye and said, "It's cancer, it's in the lymphs, but it hasn't spread anywhere else."

It hadn't spread. If my husband, Lee, hadn't cuddled me on that day, and my GP hadn't been her awesome self, and I didn't live in the UK with the most EXCELLENT NHS, it could have been a different story. Because the beastie was definitely on its way out of breast central. But, for now, I felt like one of the lucky ones.

It hadn't spread.

He said one other thing I remember...

"We are treating you with curative intent."

And I went home. Really home. I told my children, and prepped for a very tough year.

-Louisa Trunks

I Lie Unnaturally Still

I lie unnaturally still
Hands over my head
Strapped to the table, naked
Strapped at the elbow
Strapped at the wrist
Strapped at the waist
Hands in tight fists.

And if you think this is a piece of erotica,
you couldn't be further from the truth.

These straps hold me unnaturally still
So laserbeams can hit the tattoos that they gave me,
So laserbeams can strike the areas with cancer debris,
So laserbeams can scorch my skin,
And blister my breast,
And set my femininity afire, literally.
Pink dermis to puffy swell,
Bloodiness, raw meat unwell.

I lie unnaturally still
With my hands over my head
On a skinny table, naked.
The thermostat on the wall flashes 58 degrees,
Meatlocker freeze,
Shivering knock knees,

With a metal bar behind my back.
Let me say that again,
With a metal bar behind my back,
My chest pushed out,
Backbending curve,
So there is no doubt
Where those lasers will serve.

I lie unnaturally still
With my hands over my head
On a skinny table, naked,
In a deep freeze,
With a metal bar behind my back,
While lasers scorch
My diseased breasts,
And she says,
"Take a deep breath in,
Breathe in a lil' bit more,
Let out a count of four,
Keep holding,
Keep holding,
Keep holding..."
Until I can't hold anymore.
My core crumbling,
Words stumbling,
As I whisper to myself,
"Please, it hurts..."
Tears running paths down my face,

Unable to brush them away,
My silhouette they trace.

I lie unnaturally still
With my hands over my head
On a skinny table, naked.
Shivering from the icy air,
With a metal bar behind my back,
Shuddering as I hold my breath in.
For half hour a day,
Six weeks straight,
So I can live another day.
To radiation I pray,
You suit-up while naked I lay.

I lie unnaturally still.

-Joely A. Serino

Victorious

Cancer touched me
Death came banging at my door
Peeking out, lifting up my arm
Can still feel a strain
My life was once filled
with unimaginable pain
Touched on my right side
Emotions were hard to contain
I felt it and decided I'd fight this with pride
You swooped in with your wings and horns
I was looking all forlorn
Telling me all these imaginative things
You pricked me
Saturated with your venom
It made my skin turn black
The torture of it was indescribable
You hid your attack
Empathy you did lack
With your horns twirled into hooks
Giving me evil looks
When trying to push you away
You reach for me, begging me to stay
You need me to grow
A leech sucking my blood
Vampire like teeth you did show
Sinking into my soul
I couldn't see beyond

your all encompassing wingspan
I was losing control
There was darkness all around
Couldn't hear any other sounds
Your voice calling out to me
I felt immovable
Stuck in your game
There you were lurking
Glowing like those fish
in the depths of the sea
The ones with the snares
that look so enticing
Get too close and they will devour you fast
Loving them would never last
I fell into a deep sleep
You didn't ever try to wake me
You're manipulative
and only looking out for yourself
Trying to defile me, such a malicious creep
Touching me is where you felt
you had your wealth
deep inside my torso
It was shattered
You reached into my lymph nodes and muscle
Into my fresh meat
I would not admit defeat
If you went any further
I'd breathe you into my lungs
If that happens there was no turning back

Yet I caught you in time
Pull your hand off me, you lost
I'm pushing you away
In the dark you will stay
Hiding in the shadows
Waiting for another free ride
You tried to consume me
You got deep inside
Yet, I cut you out,
Replaced the cavity with my own flesh
Now I'm filled with happiness
These scars I'm left with
remind me of the war
Swelling comes and goes
Yet, I'm a fighter
Everyone knows
Slink back into your moldy cave
awaiting someone else
You are lost into the unknown
Your true colors have been shown
Can't touch me anymore
It doesn't matter what you do
I'll always beat you
It's the end and it's glorious
I came out victorious

-Gina Carrillo, Black Widow

A Hole in the Sole

The sole of my shoe lets water thru

My feet get wet, sore and blue

I wonder what I should do?

I'll polish the leather so they look shiny and new

Then no-one will know there's a hole in my sole

I could visit the cobbler

For a patch on my shoe,

Then the world will think they're brand new

The hole in my sole will always be there

But no one else knows what's inside my shoe

I'll keep my sole hidden firmly from view

So, next time you see shoes shiny and new,

Remember a hole in the sole

could be hiding from you!

-poem & photography by Diane Leopard

Pink Storm

Friday, August 13th
Never been superstitious
A routine mammogram turned horror flick
Always been healthy, but now they'll say "she's sick"
I haven't cried since
No time for the "why me?"
Aggressive, triple negative breast cancer
Stop the googling
Scared is not an option
No choice but to fight

My home is like a hallmark store
Overwhelming gestures of love and support
The aroma of pink roses in the air
"Thoughts and Prayers"
Constant reminders to be strong
Positive thinking only
Well that's easier said than done
Take that back
Stop feeling sorry
This is only the beginning of my story

My dad plays the role of my angel
Timing is everything
Started chemo right away
Just like he did
Is this really happening?
The hair on my pillow tells me it's true
The mirror never lies
It hits me

Deep breaths
Now I'm the real life GI Jane, but there's no Will Smith
Seasons change from Fall to Winter
Chemo side effects in full bloom
Christmas who? I don't know her
Weekly treatments are now a norm
Plenty of pink blankets to keep me warm
Women, young and old, fill the room
You can see it in their eyes
So tired, but they're still fighting
It's what keeps me going
I'm so inspired

2/2/22 etched in my mind
Sitting in that chair for the last time
Messages of congratulations
Don't get distracted
There is still work to do
I can see the finish line, but I'm stumbling my way
through
Testing my patience
Finally some good news
But always waiting on perfection
Collecting the scars
Proud that I made it this far

-Gia Graziano

Linda Mari

-artwork by
Kristina
Smith

On "Medical PTSD"

She protected me.
The day's events could've rocked my world,
could've broken me down beyond repair,
but she protected me.

Like taking a bottle of white-out to paper,
like taking a wet sponge to chalkboard,
like taking a pink pencil eraser to miscalculations,
she erased that day,
wiped it clean from my memory,
cleared it from my internal storage,
dumped it all out, leaving only residue;
the smallest bits and pieces,
a flash here, a word there.

The rest...I don't remember it,
no matter how hard I try.
I've looked around every turn of my brain,
in every crevice,
and that day...
it's gone
because she protected me.

-Joely A. Serino

And So, She Did

A sound she thought she'd never hear.
The echo of the doctor's voice saying
Metastatic Breast Cancer.
And in that very moment she knew
she had to fight.
And so,
she did.

Every day, twice a day,
I changed the bandages
and cleaned the wound
she was so ashamed of.
And every day, twice a day,
she had to face the reality
that this was her life now.

Surgical dressings
with tiny glittering strands
sewn into the cotton,
our little silver linings.
Mepilex bandages
and barrier spray.
The smell of Medihoney,
rubber gloves,
and infection.
The feel of cold, sterile water

running over her raw skin
as she bit down on a wash rag
through the pain of debridement.
She didn't have to let me help.
But I begged her to please
let me do this for you,
let me help you.
And so,
she did.

There were times
when she didn't know
which was worse,
the cancer or the treatment.
All the appointments,
the medications,
and the hospital visits.
Her weeks felt so busy,
yet so empty.
Monday: Wound care
Wednesday: Chemo
Friday: Oncology
And for what?
A little more time with
a growing mountain of pain.
She didn't know
if she was strong enough.
But as soon as she looked

at her two beautiful daughters,
and her precious grandbaby,
she knew she had to find
the strength to keep going,
no matter the pain.
And so,
she did.

Until she couldn't anymore.
Until MRSA took over.
Until the cancer spread further.
Until her strength was gone.
Until she knew it was time.

And in the end,
I shed my selfishness.
I wore my crown of grief
and told her she didn't
have to hold on anymore.
That it was ok to let go.
And so,
on a peaceful Monday morning,
she did.

-For Kim Johnson 6/15/1964 - 3/17/2014
by Jillian Calahan

Breast Cancer

by Lasell Jaretzki Bartlett

Has taken from me:

Sense of immortality. Doubts about my
desire to live a long life.
Approximately 10% of my left breast.
Nonchalance about mortality.
Denial about the prevalence of cancer.
Inflated sense of individual importance.
Eleven lymph nodes.
Delusions of invincibility.
Rigidity about living without drugs.
Ability to work forty hours a week.
A good deal of hair.
Ability to pay off student loans as fast as I
want to. Sensation under my left arm.
All my accrued flextime.
Willingness to pretend about my values.
Enjoyment of chocolate.
Tolerance for what doesn't genuinely interest
me. Trust in food, water, air.
Energy to work two part-time jobs.
Isolation from my true friends.
Willingness to postpone
the joys of life.

Has given me:

Acute appreciation of life, of the
here and now. Time to meditate.
Renewed sense of humor.
A kick in the butt. Yoga.
A thousand fears, a million tears.
Gratitude of health insurance.
Love of cold apples, miso soup.
Clarity and understanding of other
people's challenges. Impetus
to redefine priorities. A compelling
reason to slow down. Time to paint.
Two and a half journals of writing, to date.
New scars. New pains. Time to dream.
Some trust in doctors.
Reconnection to my intuition, to my
love of dancing. Time to read.
Determination to walk, swim, run,
to breathe deeply. Scuba lessons.
Hours of reflection. Urge to eat lots
and lots of Super Blue Green Algae.
Clarity about my responsibility to
monitor my health. New impetus to explore,
to embrace nurturing opportunities.
Sense of now or never.
Courage to wear bright colors to work.
Opportunities to say no, I can't, I won't.
Diminishing guilt about saying no,
I can't, I won't.
Fantasies of shocking people.
Lots of time with my feline friends.
Unending support
of friends and family.

lump... mammogram... needle biopsy... lumpectomy & axillary node dissection... confirmation of cancer diagnosis... reexcision... chemotherapy now... radiation later... then???

Navigating Fertility After Cancer

While most people would say getting a cancer diagnosis was the worst moment of their life, for me it was hearing the words, "You may never be able to have children." For young women facing a cancer diagnosis, fertility is many times overlooked by the care team but can be devastating to the patient. So how can you advocate for yourself and maintain hope when the future for a family is so uncertain?

Motherhood served as the compass for my life for as long as I could remember. I always loved children, and I dedicated my education and my first career to bettering the lives of young ones. These activities and passions moved me towards my goal of motherhood. Then I was diagnosed with triple positive breast cancer out of the blue at age 27.

At the time of my diagnosis, the grief and fear over not being able to have children was more monumental than the grief over losing parts of my body, going through chemotherapy, or any of the other emotional & physical trauma I would later undergo. I was suddenly fighting for my life, and the motherhood goals on which I based my entire being and self-worth were wrenched from me in an instant. I grieved for the life I had planned and the dreams I was forced to put on hold. I was reeling. How could I define myself without the future we'd planned waiting for us around the corner?

Luckily, my doctors recognized the urgency of my fertility concerns and guided us through fertility preservation options. We chose to freeze embryos, though it was expensive, and we had to rely on family for support. Many women are not afforded this option due to cost or being rushed into treatment.

After the IVF cycle, I was forced to put my dreams of motherhood aside and make a conscious decision to focus on other areas of my life for the next few years while I began hormone blocking therapy. The frozen embryos represented all the hope I had for our future family, and I had to cling to that hope while also learning how to redefine purpose and fulfillment in my life.

The next year was filled with grief, sadness, anger, and jealousy. Everyone around us seemed to be moving forward. They were getting pregnant, having babies, and planning for the future. We were held back and left behind.

As much as I wanted to be happy for them, it was soul-crushing. The unfairness of my cancer diagnosis and subsequent life changes brought me so much anger. As I examined my anger, I realized it was rooted in fear. Who was I without the ability to have children? Would my marriage sustain? How would I find purpose in life without the goal of motherhood driving me forward? I wish I could say I had a grand epiphany or a magic moment that helped me move forward from this discomfort, yet the truth is far from it.

I did realize that, while I was caught up grieving my future as a mother, I was missing out on opportunities to live and thrive. I began journaling regularly. It helped, and I continued to build my blog. I found ways to give back to the breast cancer community. And I slowly took back control of my life. Little by little, I began to define myself as a leader, a writer, an advocate, and a community-builder. It was through this transformation that I came to love myself on a deeper level. I was so much more than a woman without children. I was still worthy!

I gradually stopped thinking about babies nonstop and began dedicating that time and emotion to rediscovering myself, bonding with my husband, and fostering my passions. We made time to travel. We built two businesses from the ground up, and we redefined our goals as a couple.

As I grew emotionally and professionally, I also redefined my meaning of success. And it was no longer limited to my ability to become a mother. I still wanted a family, but I began to see the future much differently. Maybe it would take many years. Maybe we would adopt. Maybe we would use a surrogate. I knew that I would be a mother someday, even if it was not how I originally imagined it. I was truly happy and fulfilled for many years without motherhood as my driving force.

Then my biological clock set in. In the fall of 2018, I had been on my hormone blocking medication for almost 3 years, and I was ready to revisit the discussion of taking a break. My husband and I weighed the risks and the rewards and decided it was time. We were not getting any younger, and there was no data or research showing a benefit of waiting 5 years vs. 3 years. I also started finding more and more stories of women like me having children after cancer around that time frame. Luckily my oncologist supported our decision and like a floodgate, the desires, dreams, and fears came streaming out of the box I had locked away. There were no guarantees, but we would hope for my cycle to return, and then we would explore our options. The two-year countdown began.

In the months that would follow, I would conceive naturally and lose both the baby and my right fallopian tube in an emergency surgery that threatened to break my hope and my life. We would try again naturally without success and begin the process of a frozen embryo transfer later in the fall, this time jaded and fearful. When those two blue lines appeared, we were cautiously optimistic but took it day by day. By 6 weeks, we couldn't contain our joy and shared the news with our families. We spent the holidays filled with joy celebrating this miracle with our family and headed back to an ultrasound two days after Christmas. For the first time, I allowed myself to think about the future – a future where I was a mother.

The technician turned on the machine, and we were chattering with excitement, ready to hear the heartbeat…but suddenly the room got quiet. There was no sound. No heartbeat. "Maybe it's just too early," they said. "Come back in a few days, and we'll check again." We drove home in silence, the truth already sinking in. It was over again; I could feel it. Our baby was gone. I couldn't leave the couch; I couldn't be alone! Alone was too scary as the reality flooded my psyche. We laid and cried and held one another for hours. This couldn't be happening again.

After my D&C and another surgery that followed, we were back in the fertility specialist's office, this time unsure where to turn. Were we out of options? The cancer clock was ticking each day, threatening me to return to hormone blocking therapy in less than a year.

We went to couples' therapy and were beginning the steps to come to terms with our new reality. We had time for only one more FET (frozen embryo transfer), and then we would need to wait 2-3 more years before trying again. The next FET hinged on my hormone levels returning to normal, but week after week they were too high. I began to get frustrated, every day, time slipping away.

I started thinking ahead preparing for the worst. I began to explore surrogacy and adoption more seriously. I filled my time talking to other cancer survivors and parents who had started families through alternate methods, and I kept hearing a common theme. Once you hold that child in your arms, it doesn't matter how you got there. Exploring the options brought me comfort and reassurance that there was still hope for us. I knew I was meant to be a mother, even if the path or the means was not as I had imagined.

After back to back blood tests showing my levels were still too high, my husband turned to me and said, "I think you're pregnant." I dismissed him nonchalantly. The idea felt so far-fetched; we weren't even trying. To appease him, I peed on a stick and went downstairs for breakfast. When I came back, he held up the stick and said, "You're pregnant," but the words didn't register. After almost 2 years of trying, there was no way it happened by "accident," but bloodwork confirmed it was true. Our little rainbow baby was due in December 2019. I was mentally preparing for another marathon ahead and still healing from my miscarriage, but my body was 2 steps ahead of me growing this precious baby.

In this odd twist of irony, it wasn't until I let myself imagine a future without carrying a child, that this child was conceived. Now as a mother, I see that everything I went through prepared me to be a better, more patient, and relaxed parent for my son. The path to his arrival, while riddled with loss and pain, demonstrated that I was stronger than I ever knew. The moment I held him in my arms, my journey to get to that point no longer mattered. While the memory of my losses will never go away, my son Mason brings such joy to me and the world, that it overpowers my pain and allows me to grow and thrive.

If you are on your own fertility journey after cancer, know that you are not alone, and even in your darkest moments, there is hope to be found.

-Anna Crollman, My Cancer Chic

The Cancer Rollercoaster

Buckle up

You're shoved on

You've no choice

You've no control

You're in the hands of the machine

The anxiety kicks in on the first climb

Then you're off

Highs and lows

Tears and fears

Going around again and again

Tugging at the seatbelt

If you're lucky

The bars will lift and you can climb out

But mentally

You're never getting off

This ride

-Sally Martin

A Mantra

I can get through this. I will get through this. I can get through this. I will get through this.

-Joely A. Serino

Restless

Rest up - they say

Relax and enjoy your day

How can I do that after my op?

When restless leg sensations are making me hop

I'm trying to sleep in my bed at night

I'm trying to rest up to continue the fight

Fears run through my head...

Is it DVT? Need to keep moving

I'm drinking lots of water...Is it improving?

Lying on my back is not ideal...

My breast needs no pressure for it to heal.

I'm so tired, I must recover

I need to keep succeeding as a wife and a mother.

Too many questions...Is my blood pressure up?

Too many thoughts overfilling my cup.

Twitch, kick, toss and turn,

These legs! It's sleep I want; can they just not learn!

I watch TV in the early hours of the morn,

The room gets lighter as the sun starts to dawn.

I go for a walk, a soak in the bath,

I sit in the garden, then de-weed the path.

I hope these ideas work to get some sleep,

If not I'll do yoga or a meditation technique.

In the dead of night, as my husband snores,

Getting louder and louder, the sound just bores...

Into my head that is wide awake.

WIDE AWAKE for goodness sake!

I WANT TO SLEEP

I WANT TO REST

TO GET BACK TO THE NORM

OF A LIFE WORTH LIVING AND NOT SO TORN...

Apart from cancer and my RESTLESS sleep.

DEEP BREATHS...

and.........................

RELAAAAXXX.

-Kathryn Bassett

On "Survivorship"

Receiving the devastating news,
hearing those ominous words,
I immediately put my head down,
sealed my eyes closed,
firmly clenched my jaw,
and did the work to survive.
Day in, day out,
a warrior on a lethal path,
determination in my blood,
hands in closed fists,
ready for my invisible opponent.
Failure wasn't an acceptable option;
victory was to be mine.
And now I'm a "survivor."
"No evidence of disease," they exclaimed.
Smiles on their festive faces,
family & friends threw confetti in the air.

So I safely stepped into the morning sunshine,

lifted my heavy head after all this time,

opened my tired, pale eyes, & softened my tender jaw.

Because I thought the work was done.

I survived, didn't I?

But a shattering of reality that the task at hand was just

beginning,

a sobering realization of the trauma that my heart just

weathered,

an intense awareness that I will NEVER be the same

again,

sucked me back into the darkness;

a black hole in the land of survivorship where I still

dwell.

A newborn baby,

all hands and feet flailing,

a new version of me

that will one day be set free

from the ashes of healing.

-Joely A. Serino

We Had To Be

Chapter 3:

To

For our family & friends,
for those who suffered,
for those who caused
the suffering...

"Cancer hurts the hearts
of those who fight from
the sidelines."

-unknown

We Had To Be

Inheritance

She loved to bake
And she loved to wear sarees
She loved gardening
And raising plants and animals
Along with humans
Her home was filled with
Chickens and dogs
Food and family
Fruit trees and herbs of all kinds
She loved creating and nurturing things

I never met my grandmother
She died a few months before I was born
All I heard about her
Was from my mother
Who was expecting a child
While losing a parent
Caught in the cycle of life
Birth and death coinciding
Trapped between joy and despair

I don't know what to call her
Nana, granny, grandma
Are alien words to me when I
Think and talk about her
Because I never got to use them
When I was younger, I called her mama
Because that's what my mother called her
And I thought that's what she as known as
Now I just refer to her by her name

That's all I have of my grandmother —
A name
And memories passed on by my mother
Which are actually her memories of a mother
I have no memories of her as a grandmother
Losing hair, tiredness, whittling away
Cancer took away a person I never met or knew
And yet she lives in me
She loved to knit
My mother prefers crochet
I learned both knitting and crochet in school
And never took up either since then

Last week I knitted a scrunchie
Everyone said it was bright and beautiful
And intricate and inspiring
For a first attempt at knitting after decades
And I remembered my grandmother
Because my mother does not knit
How did the scrunchie turn out so well?
Her talents must run through me
Her genes met me, even though she didn't

I have no choice over which genes have passed on to me
Sewing and baking and gardening run in the family
As do cancerous cells that demand regular checkups
My mother needs to do them
And so do I
And my grandmother lives on
In the annual hospital visits
In the yearly family get togethers
In every medical history chart and report
In every knit and purl winding around a needle
In every cake fresh from the oven
That's my inheritance
From a person I never met or knew
-Renata Pavrey

Dear 2020

Thank you. You have, without doubt, been a monumental bitchface. Toe curlingly, mind bendingly, 'holy moly surely not more'- ingly, fucking AWFUL. But, you have taught me more than any other year, and for that you at least get my respect, a begrudging doff of my cap as I kick the gate shut on your long cruel path.

Sometimes our best teachers aren't the kind ones. They are the ones who make us stand in the cold, watching the warm gurgle of life through someone else's window. The ones who make us go back up the mountain when the first time took everything we thought we had. The ones who smile kindly, point to the back of the room, and say 'again', 'again', 'again'. And boy, did you employ all these tactics and more!

I have spent this afternoon in my favourite place, with one of my favourite people. My hill, my solace, my sanatorium. It never disappoints. As the sun went down, it brought an unintentional poignancy. A profound tearful close, as I realized it was over, and that despite the bitterness, there has been much sweetness.

2020, thank you for teaching me to be still. How to curl into myself and hold on, how to brace through a storm. Whilst ravaged by the torrent, I found more strength than I needed. I learned that I, like all humans, have a miraculous ability to control my experience by altering my perception. Life is only bad when I allow it to be. Sometimes I am still taken by surprise when people refer to me as ill, or when fatigue flattens me, or when I look in the mirror and see my aged, worn face. 2020, you have taught me how far determined positivity can take me.

You also taught me to move. Whenever I can, because I can. Make that heart pound, push on up that hill, step out into that sun. Because, there is nothing that I need more than physical and mental health....

...except love. And that, my affably villainous friend, has quite probably been your biggest lesson. The soul-nourishing light that   shines from my children's laughing eyes, the healing warmth that envelops me along with each embrace, the small zap of happy-energy that buzzes through me with every kindness. The immense feeling of power that comes from being part of the tsunami of love and public gratitude. The quiet peace that comes from private gratitude and self-love. These things are my treasures. These are the things I would save in a house fire. I could see these things before, but 2020, you taught me their true value and one simple truth: you give out love and kindness, and you get it back in spades (as long as you are paying attention).

2020, you shined a spotlight on my freedom, our NHS, and my privilege. I owe each a great debt, which I will repay through gratitude. And you taught me unequivocally that I don't ever want to homeschool, even for all the gold in gringotts, and that there is more to teaching English than the cute, alliterative phrase 'heinous penis.'

So, as the sun goes down, thank you. Would I change you? Nah. Am I glad you came? Probably. Would I invite you back for more tea? Not a hope. You are banned. See ya, thanks for your efforts. Now fuck off and make way for your kinder, cancer-free sister, 2021. I have a feeling we are going to be great friends.

Yours Sincerely,
Louisa Trunks
Breast Cancer Survivor

-writing & photography by Louisa Trunks

A Love Letter to Cancer

Dear Cancer,
You have taught me so much.
You have taught me that even when I think I have nothing left,
when I think I have expended all of my strength,
and will power, and resiliency,
and have nothing left to fight with,
I still have more.
There is a fire burning deep inside of me that cannot be
extinguished with just tears alone.
I am strong because of you.
And while you may have hardened some of my soft parts,
I have learned to love the little things and all that's left of me.
You have taught me that being fearless sometimes means
facing your fears head-on.
It means admitting when you are afraid.
It means not giving up when that is all you want to do.
You've taught me that my people are the ones who reach in
when I cannot reach out.
You've taught me that I cannot do everything on my own,
and you've taught me that in order to heal,
I need to get out of my comfort zone and embrace this new
version of myself.
Because no matter what,
she is beautiful.

-Joely A. Serino

You

YOU crept silently into my life
YOU came along without warning
No lights flashing, no sirens
screaming
Are YOU real or am I dreaming?
YOU turned my world upside down
As only YOU can do
The lights went dim, my head was spinning
I didn't know if YOU were winning.

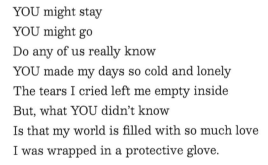

YOU might stay
YOU might go
Do any of us really know
YOU made my days so cold and lonely
The tears I cried left me empty inside
But, what YOU didn't know
Is that my world is filled with so much love
I was wrapped in a protective glove.

YOU changed my world but that's not bad
For every day I feel so glad
The beauty that surrounds us all
Was waiting just outside the door
YOU held my life in your cold hand
But YOU gave my world a loving glow.

If YOU should ever call again
I'll walk with YOU into the rain
But just for now we walk together
Your shadow never far away
YOU may come, YOU may go
YOU may take and YOU may hurt
BUT, just for now I want to say
Thank YOU for giving me a bright new day.

-poem & photography by Diane Leopard

An Apology to My Mum

*Three years before my Mum was diagnosed with breast cancer, I lost my Dad - her husband - to lung cancer. One year before her diagnosis, cancer also took my father-in-law. -Sarah Fawcett

I will never forget that feeling of dread

As you spoke those four little words

The thoughts raced through my head

Time dilated and blurred

Oh, how I loathe that hateful word

Too far away to support or assist

The fear of death, of further loss, persisted

But there was nothing I could do

Were we going to lose you too?

We got lucky this time

The lump found early, still curable

Averting the lingering spectre of 'terminal'

But I feel like I owe you an apology

I wasn't there for you as much as I should've been

Unable to face the fear again

I couldn't cope with the reality

Of another threat to the existence of my family.

Still waiting for the next hammer to fall

I avoided the in-depth details

Or erased them all from my memory?

I don't recall the journey you went through

I know you had others there for you

But that didn't include me

And for that, I am truly sorry.

-Sarah Fawcett

Dearest Birgit,

First of all, I'm so pissed that you left me here. Your mere existence gave my life shape and security. Being ten years older than me, you were like a second mom. Now, I am all alone.

Going to your house that night to get your pups nearly killed me. Did you see me there looking around? I couldn't believe what I saw; your pain and suffering was everywhere. These images haunt me. Why didn't you tell me? I wanted to give you space to live your way, not mine.

I know you wanted to keep my life as normal as possible in the shadow of your pain.

Your babies were skin and bones, and all three ran into one carrier. Thankfully two immediately found a home, but the mean one made sure no one would adopt him. I swear the little shit smiled after people came by to see him foam at the mouth. I'm thinking that was your grand plan, letting me have this lunatic dog to help me deal with you dying. I almost couldn't write that word, dying. He became the love of my life. I tried to make up for all the things I should've done for you with him. Stupid, huh?

Anyway, I want you to know how important you are to me, and I hope you still get my texts. Thank you for trying to protect me from your undeniable suffering. You spent your life protecting me, and at what cost?

I never told you, but I always wanted to be a free spirit, just like you. That I wanted to be an artist, just like you. The things you thought were your weaknesses were strengths in my eyes; I just never told you that.

I could never survive having (rectal) cancer, an ostomy bag, breast cancer, and trying to work, live, and simply put one foot in front of the other. You are my hero. Still and forever.

Birgit, I hope our dog has found his way back to you and that you see me painting in the garden.

I am and will always be your sister.

Love you Ditty,
Roachie

-Karin Hammler

And just like that,

the heavy clouded curtains have lifted

from my sunken, deadened eyes,

And the hologrammed light

shines over my long-legged lashes.

And as my eyelids open...

All I see is love.

Just pure love from all directions.

*A dedication to the town of Bogota, NJ
for all that they did for my family and I
during my breast cancer journey
-Joely A. Serino

One Last Anthurium

Honoring my mom's long fight against breast cancer with her favorite flower, the Anthurium.
Te iubesc, Mama.

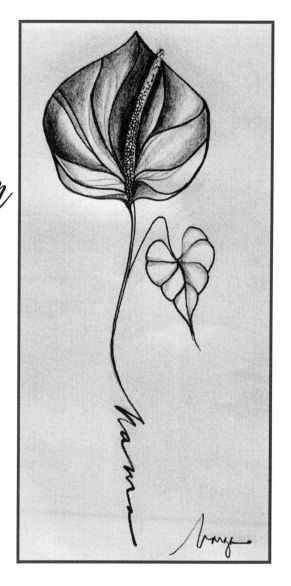

-artwork and inscription by Marga (Alexandra Colta)

December 6th, 2021

Claudia said......
Don't do anything for 5 years.
I should have listened to Claudia
But I know so much more now
Something new, how to get through to something new

A tragedy told through song?
A transformation revealed through movement?
A comedy that blasts cold white light on the horror?

An ode to my lost breast. My lost self. So that my Phoenix rises from the ashes; I rise from the ashes.

Too much?

But, oh, so true.

How do we do that? Flash into flame and then rise again from the smoldering ashes, to become something new?

Photos of women/scars

A band that plays with me, responds to me
- a rock musical?
- A mournful ballet?
- African drums bringing my heart back with their rhythmic hold?

Breaking free from the binds that once held the frame of me together, to be loosed into nothingness- swaying about/held only by the compression of the water, to emerge from the drug state that kept me from losing my mind altogether, to find the strength of my legs and abs and arms and chest as I swish through the chlorine.
5 years. I should have listened to Claudia.

And now that I'm here, well, almost on June 1, 2022, I almost loathe to return to the beginning, to the before. I feel my desire to just move forward.

But, first:
To remember.
To reflect.
To reframe the narrative, not as a tragedy, but yes it was it is oh fuck I miss my boob and my hair!

To claim the rediscovery of me.

And oh, don't you just love breasts?! I do. I dooooooooo!
While I mourned and longed for the curve and slope of the
old me, I began noticing the absolute beauty of breasts all
around me. Not in sexual objectification, but in keen sensual
awareness of shape and build/slope and valley. Strength and
beauty. Art.

I am a docent?
A fanatic collector, but without a full collection?

Oh yes, look at you! To hold the softness of you! The fullness
of you!

(A barrage of images: breasts of every shape and color,
clothed and in movement- focus not on the faces but on the
shapes)

And then there is me. The image of me reflected back to my
brain, translating the loss and horror to despair and scar to
finally strength and grace? and dare I say flair? Even sexy?
A uniboobed, scarred, takes no fucks fury, that lights the
light inside me again?

(A barrage of images of me? Topless? In movement?)

Yup. I think so.

A chorus of women. You can't get through
this without the women- they
reflect/affirm/comfort/support/KNOW.

a chorus of dancers- to move as I feel

A band

Me

Moving scrims for projections and shadow play

Physical improv- a dancer moves me as a marionette
might, as a lover might bringing me to the heights of
orgasm and release

We are the champions.

-Stephanie Burlington Daniels

Ode to My Right Breast

All week, after surgery, I carried you
in my hand, cradled you, hot swollen
beast, but now I must let you go,
bequeath you to the surgeon's slick
slender blade, to the space time
continuum of dissection and
formaldehyde suspension, bequeath
you to the universe of cellular
breakdown, the land of necrosis,
to the science of recovery,
of carrying forward, of imbalance
and asymmetry. I say goodbye to you,
my right breast, as we part ways
at this unexpected time. I thank you
for the blessing of being part of me,
for the blessing of holding within you
the seed of my tumultuous nature
that now must be set free, for the
darkness that you held cradled
in a place safe from the rest of my
body. I thank you and release you as
I build a new carapace out of chaos,
out of loss. I release you, release you.

-Laura L. Hansen

An Ode to Medical Marijuana

And as I inhale her

pain-free pleasantries,

I can feel each bubble

that surrounds my

sickened cells

burst in relief;

an effervescence of the body,

that pop-pop of a satisfying punch into bubble wrap.

The poison disappears into the atmosphere,

steam rising into my airspace over a quaking boil,

sparks flickering skyward over a raging fire,

and I am

free.

-Joely A. Serino

Flowers on my Window Sill

A special nurse did a kind gesture for me when I was down & ill,
She picked beautiful flowers from her garden & placed them on
my window sill,
I always felt comfortable knowing I was in her care,
She took the time to listen & reassured me when I was scared,
She showed me compassion & concern when I was in need,
Colleen took the extra step to show this by her thoughtful deed.

-Lori Fischer

Dear Colleen,

I want you to know how much I appreciated the care you gave me
when I was in the hospital. I always felt like I was in confident &
compassionate hands. I'll never forget how you took the time to
listen & reassure me when I was afraid of getting the IV in my
left arm where they took lymph nodes out.

I still have the jar the flowers were in because it is a nice
reminder that a special person came into my life at a time of need.

Thank you for everything,
Lori

Victorious

To all those who think it would never happen to them;

 it definitely could

To all those who think breast cancer is just for women; it's not

To all those who no longer feel beautiful;

you have no idea how radiant you are

To all those who are terrified of the future;

it's okay to be scared, but don't let it paralyze you

To all those fighting this never ending war;

you are stronger than you think

To all those who want to give up; don't.

You've come way too far

To all those who can't talk about it; it's okay.

We're here when you're ready

To all those who think they're alone; you're not.

We're here for you

This battle is relentless, but you are resilient

The fear never stops. You are not your diagnosis, and you are

not alone

We are here to fight with you, we are your ears to listen, your

shoulder to cry on, and your army for battle

Together we shall be victorious

-S.A. Lucero

"And if time were to stall, I could never tell it all, words are few, this will have to do.
I just want to thank you."
—Maverick City Music

Fierce

Yes, cancer scared me, took my breath away, kept me from much needed sleep, and made me probably not as polite as I normally am. That shadow of fear hanging over me like a darkness so thick you have to keep blinking your eyes to try and see.

However, this is not the first time I have been afraid. I have battled with fear throughout my life, and I have learned who my weapon is. He, my God, stands right next to me every day and in my place when I can't, and He surrounds me with love and friendship.

My fears were met by an army of friends that were strong when I couldn't be. The unexpected blessing in allowing yourself to be loved and taken care of. Gosh that's hard. My friends that have taken such good care of me have been more generous than I could have ever imagined, made me laugh, kept me moving, and my family fed. It has been such an overwhelming feeling of love that I could never explain it. The bitter was replaced by the sweet and turned into thankfulness.

These drawings were done while I was in bed recuperating from breast cancer. I am not a very good patient. I get bored easily then start feeling sorry for myself, and I can only watch so much Netflix. Fortunately, my girlfriends showed up. They called, they came over, they brought food and gifts, they cleaned my house, and they made me laugh. One day, bored out of my mind, I thought, maybe I should tap into the artist in me. Since I couldn't exercise my body, I should probably exercise my mind. So I asked my son to bring me his sketch pad and his colored pencils. These drawings are the result. A representation of the women in my life and the essence of them that affected me most. They are a thank you note to the beautiful women in my life. While these drawings may represent the friends in my life and the battle I was fighting, I also know that they represent friends in your life too. Whether good times or bad, life is always more fun with a friend.

-Michelle Lutjen,
The Thankful Tulip blog

Inspire

Grace

Blossom

Rise

Peace

Artwork by Michelle Lutjen

Radiated

First, they measured me and
put me through a machine
to simulate being radiated.
Then they drew crude x's
on my body with Sharpies
and tattooed three dots
into my chest.
And if that was not enough,
They put stickers onto my ribs,
drew marks on those too.

Silent tears streamed down
the sides of my face:
I felt devalued,
like I didn't matter,
as if I were so insignificant
that someone found the need
to scribble onto my flesh,
like I was less than,
less than anyone.

Now, I'd been cut open,
excised thrice.
A port was carved into
the right side of my chest
and through that port,
I'd been pumped full
of drugs that killed
fast-growing cancer cells.
My hair fell out.
My fingernails turned
dark and thick.
Chemicals stole my thoughts,
my concentration,
robbed snatches of my brain
that I might never get back.
They turned my piss
bright orange.
They made my bodily fluids
toxic for forty-eight hours.
But still,
I'd never felt
as violated as when
I'd been radiated.

-Cathy Gigante-Brown

Frankenstein

Dear Dr. Frankenstein,
Make me please into Art, a Masterpiece, a Beautiful creature,
There is a spark in my being, beware for I am fearless, and
therefore powerful

Today this hole will be filled in my chest, although I'll never be
the same,
I requested thee maker from my clay to mold me, woman
I did solicit thee from darkness to promote me, pardoning my
outward form,
There is a science of building a woman out of fragments of
little light

We are fashioned creatures, but half made up
I will pioneer a new life to explore,
unknown powers are unfolding to the world, the deepest
mysteries of creation
I myself am entirely made of flaws, stitched together with good
intentions,
just trying to get through this thing called life

We could all die any day, but before I'll let that happen, I'll dance my life away

The beginning is always today, I may look different but my soul remains

It is now ever stronger, my resilience has brought me through this

My life has taken an amazing transformation

Thank you doctor for everything, I look forward to what the next day brings

-Gina Carrillo, Black Widow

Dear Cancer,

You're always in the back of my mind
Unforgettable
Like a lost love
But there's no love here
I don't want you back
Broken hearts everywhere
Life's toughest teacher
Turning fears into lessons

You probably think I'm weak
But your presence only makes me stronger
The joke's on you
Dealt this hand for a reason
I always play to win
Poker face with fear filled eyes
Striving to look at the bright side
I don't want to just survive
I want to LIVE
Screaming from rooftops
The sound is deafening
Can you hear me?

Go ahead, take my hair
It doesn't define me
My beauty comes from within
You can take my breasts too
They tried to kill me
Peeling back the layers of insecurity
Forcing me into vulnerability
Pushing me to be courageous
A WARRIOR
A SURVIVOR
And for that, I thank you

-Gia Graziano

The Red-Devil Dragon Slayer

*An ode to Adriamycin, a bright red chemotherapy,
nicknamed "The Red Devil," commonly used for Breast Cancer

Panic on their pallid faces,
At the syllables spoken in her name,
Her reputation scares the gutsiest,
When hope plays a hide-and-seek game.

The infamous "Red Devil" moniker,
Inciting the torture she imparts,
Is rivaled by a silken red cape
That surrounds her heavy heart.

I've spied her snipping ponytails,
Teary tendrils that she hordes,
Then defend those weeping maidens,
With the swinging of her swords.

Adept at digging under deep,
Arresting pain with all her twists,
Swimming superhighways with one shot,
Crippling ankles, knees, and wrists.

But a hand held after the pain subsides,

A tenderness for those she's maimed,

She mourns for women suffering this arduous plight,

For lost battles and bodies claimed.

And even when heavily surrounded,

Ancestral shadows in the rearview,

The blood may rise about the lines;

She's the destiny I was due.

"To save you is to hurt you,"

The ultimate curse she must carry.

Dreaded tears spring in dire anticipation

From the idol and adversary.

So I take her in, my villainous hero,

My unstoppable battling betrayer.

Blowing kisses with trepid appreciation

To my Red Devil Dragon Slayer.

-Joely A. Serino

Phantom Pain

You were my demigod,
Omnipotent,
Omnipresent,
All knowing and all seeing.

Now my phantom pain,
Persistent and permeating my
very being.

I feel you like a haunting
on hallowed flesh,
Yearning for your touch.

Severed and separated
the pain has endured
and is almost too much.

A lingering essence
Heavier than the perfume
of a passing stranger.

Penetrating, preoccupying
My thoughts, a beguiling blend
of familiarity and danger.

Flashbacks of youth
Languish with yearnings,
Left unsatisfied to my core.

Carefree days corrupted,
By memories of love and
lust, lost forever more.

Reality now my bedfellow,
In wakefulness you are
my phantom pain.

Until the embers of our
yesteryears melt into dreams,
In which life begins again.

-Berny Stratton

YOU are one of a kind.

The one who watches us cry.

The one who wants us to try.

No matter where we go in life,

YOU'll always be on our mind.

YOU are not only our teacher,

YOU are our friend.

YOU're a survivor,

who didn't want it to end.

-A dedication to Joely A. Serino,
written by Kashana D. Roman,
former student & friend

To Kimmie,

My last memory of you
where your heart was still beating,
tortures me.
But if it allows me to remember
all of the good times,
I will take it.

If the feel of your cold skin
against the palm of my hand
allows me to remember
the warmth of your hugs,
I will take it.

If the sound of your death rattle
allows me to remember
the sound of your voice,
the sound of your laugh,
I will take it.

If the guilt I feel
for not being able to save you
allowed you to feel safe
and comfortable and loved,
I will take it.

I didn't want today to come.
But it does, every year.
And if it's the only way to not forget you,
I will take it.
A million times,
I will take it.

-Jillian Calahan

The Forever Letters...

To Sydney,

Her first born. Her heart. Her sunshine. You could always make her laugh. You have her sense of humor and her youthful spirit. I don't think I've ever laughed as much as I did with you guys on Fridays. Those were some of the best nights of my life and man, oh man, do I miss them. Watching you become a mom was one of the hardest but happiest times in your mom's life. She wouldn't have changed it for anything. I wish that, just one more time, I could see her give you that look, you know the one that would make you laugh so hard no sound came out! You may have given her a few gray hairs, but she was so, so proud of you, Syd.

To Destiny,

Her second born. Her soul. Her moonbeams in the dark. You have her sass and her stubbornness! One of her favorite stories to tell of you was when you were around 2 years old and climbed a bookshelf so you could eat a crayon! You've had that sass since you were born! I know she would have given anything to see that you're a mom now too. She fought so hard to stay, and you were so young when she got sick. I had asked her, at one point, to come stay with me so it would be a little easier to take care of her. But she wanted to stay at the house, because that's where you were. She wanted to make sure you'd be ok, and you will be. You will be, Tiny Boo Boos.

To Cielo,

Her first grandbaby. Her love. Her world. You, my dear girl, were her everything. She watched you come into this world and hers instantly changed. She wanted to be here so bad to watch you grow up. She talked about you all the time. About how you came into our lives at just the right time and made all the dark parts so much brighter. She loved teaching you things and was always in awe of how quickly you learned new stuff. You filled her heart with so much love, and I believe that love helped keep her here a little longer. Thank you for that.

To Elizabeth and Leviathan,

Your Grandma never got to meet you, but I can tell you this. She would have loved you to the ends of the earth and beyond the moon and stars. I'd like to think that you two are beautiful bright shooting stars that she sent to us. If ever on a spring day, you feel a warm breeze cradle your face, I wouldn't be surprised if that was her checking in, seeing how you are doing and how much you've grown. She'll always be there, watching over you and loving you, always.

-Jillian Calahan

A Letter to my Mummo (Grandma)

Mummo,

I *used* to be so mad.

I kept lying in my bed, thinking about all the moments we lost before we had a chance to experience them together. There could have been so many with our entire family together.

Why did you have to go and leave *us*?

I remember the day I got the call.

Friday the 13th.

I was on my way to surprise everyone for the holidays.

And suddenly, there was one less person to hug.

You.

Since that day, I have moved back home to Finland.

Life has been hectic, but we have all survived it the best we can.

Four years ago, I found the love of my life.

Yes, it *finally* happened.

I know you would have loved him, just like I do.

Like I said in the beginning, I *used* to be so mad.

But my heart got lighter after realizing I should focus on things we experienced together, instead of all the things we missed.

The pain never really goes away, but our memories together keep me smiling.

I was lucky to have you in my life for almost 22 years.

I remember that one Christmas when we came to visit for the holidays.

You always made your cinnamon rolls when we drove up north to see you.

My little brother loved those and was ready to eat as many as possible.

But then, that one time, you had decided to bake something else.

My brother cried, and it took a long time to get him to calm down.

And what did you do?

You woke up at the crack of dawn to bake those cinnamon rolls.

That was the memory I shared about you during the memorial service.

Not him. *Me.*

It will always be one of my favorite memories of you.

Like the time when I tried to say *kato mummo kuinka paljon murkkuja!*

(Look, grandma, how many ants!)

And it ended up sounding like *kato mummo kuinka paljon mulkkuja!*

Thanks to my speech defect, I told you to look at how many *dicks* there were instead of ants.

Your laugh that day.

Oh, what I would do to hear that again.

I remember how you started crying, as it was that funny.
And I had no idea why you reacted like you did back then.
But I remember that laugh.

When I think about it more, my favorite memory is what you
told me the last time we saw each other.
You told me to follow my dreams and never give up.
So here I am, writing and dreaming big.
I know you would have loved reading my stories, *even the ones
with spicy scenes.*

Before I forget: don't forget to hug pappa really tight.
He finally got his wish and reunited with you earlier this year.
We miss him so much, but we are happy to know you are
together.
Like it was meant to be.

Love always,
Kiira

-K.H. Anastasia

Did You Ask Her?

When her life changed in an instant, did you ask her
questions?
Did you ever let her lead?
Did you ask her how much she knew about the disease?
Did you ask her if she was ok, or what did she need?
Did you even ask her to stay, when all she wanted to do
was run away?
Did you ask her how fragile she felt, instead of telling
her she's strong?
Did you ask what her wants are?
What it looked like to care all along?
Did you ask her if it was ok for you to pretend or just
completely go away?
Did you ask her enough to help her feel safe,
 in a destroyed relationship that wasn't just yours to
break?
Did you ever ask her what ALL the disease took away?
Did you ask her how to be?
Did you ever let her lead?

*To my loves, to the world, live your life for you in order
for it to be truer than true.
-Vanessa Marie Upton

Write your own letter...

Whether it be to a loved one who was affected by cancer, your team or doctor who took care of you, your "breastie" bestie who you can always count on, to yourself telling your inner conscience how proud you are, or to the beast called "cancer," write a letter here revealing your innermost feelings and thoughts, just as so many did before you in this chapter. Keep it for yourself or share it on Instagram using the hashtag #wehadtobe.

Dear _____,

_____

_____

_____

_____

_____

_____

_____

_____

_____

_____

_____

_____

_____

_____

_____

_____

_____

_____

_____

_____

_____

_____

_____

_____

_____

_____

_____

_____

_____

_____

_____

_____

_____

_____

_____

_____

_____

_____

_____

_____

_____

_____

_____

_____

_____

_____

_____

_____

_____

_____

_____

_____

_____

Sincerely,

Chapter 4:

Be

All the things you had to be, before, during, & after breast cancer

"And once the storm is over, you won't remember how you made it through, how you managed to survive. You won't even be sure whether the storm is really over. But one thing is certain. When you come out of the storm, you won't be the same person who walked in. That's what this storm's all about."

-Haruki Murakami

We Had To Be

Cancer 24/7

The alarm goes off
After a disturbed night
I've anxiously been thinking about cancer

I get up, make some tea, put on the news
There's a breakthrough new treatment
I hopefully think about cancer

I have a shower and take a glimpse
Of my new body
And painfully think about cancer

I drive the kids to school
As we say goodbye
I think about how much I love them
And fearfully think about cancer

I take my dogs for a walk
Bump into an old friend
We exhaustively think about cancer

I decide what I should or shouldn't

Be eating for lunch

And vigilantly think about cancer

A charity appeal is on TV

As I sit and eat my lunch

I emotionally think about cancer

I nod off as I'm tired these days

I never used to feel like this before

I mournfully think about cancer

I collect the kids from school

And the mums ask how I am

We casually chat about cancer

The phone rings

Another appointment at the hospital

I logistically think about cancer

I have a flick through social media

And check up on my "breasties"

And proudly think about cancer

I make dinner and pour a glass of wine
I really shouldn't be drinking this
I guiltily think about cancer

I sit down and watch a film
One of the main characters is sick
I tearfully think about cancer

I reply to the many messages
I've received today
And repetitively think about cancer

I take my makeup off before bed
Not recognizing myself in the mirror
And angrily think about cancer

I lay down and try to go to sleep
But I struggle because, no surprise
I can't stop thinking about cancer

-Sally Martin

Warrior Cry

What if trauma made you grow
Inside me you tried to kill me
But I'm a fighter, not a quitter
You heard my shout when I said...
Get the hell out!
I didn't let you in too deep, I win
I beat you
Like a piñata
Blessings fell out
My love and support was astounding
This is such a beautiful pain
A time of transformation
I wake up thankful to live
My strength heard my inner warrior cry
I don't want to die, just yet
I danced with death,
It got scared away,
I feel the wind as I fly free
Stormy weather can't ruffle my feathers
I love my scars, I fought this war my way
As tears stream down my face, the paint stays
I'm now in a wonderful place
Whatever this world may bring
Now I know that my soul can survive anything

-Gina Carrillo, Black Widow

"I had to be tough, and I had to be strong. I had to amputate and previve and show my daughter that this gene mutation could be beaten, even though it just beat her grandma."

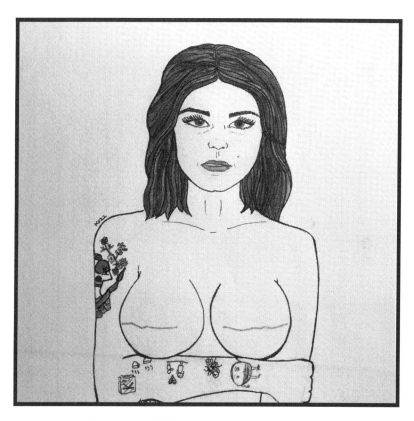

-quote and artwork by Kristina Smith

Be Still Girl

I've overdone it. I've acted like a greedy toddler who thought she could eat all the cakes, only to find herself throwing up at her own party with her mum gently rubbing her back and giving her the 'I told you so' look. There are differences – my gluttony was for life, I'm too gray to be a toddler, and my mum rubbed my back via WhatsApp – but, I'm still feeling as sulky and petulant.

Since chemo and surgery, I've gorged on 'being Louisa Trunks' again and failed to 'just be.' I've ticked all the recovery boxes, completed my wellbeing To-Do list, and totally overlooked the most important thing, rest.

My white blood count is low, I have an infection, some small wounds aren't healing well, and my mood is cranky. Thoroughly crunked in fact. I've been gently poked in the direction of the sanatorium by several folks this week, and properly booted through the doors today by one of my doctors.

If, like me, you have the modern aversion to the concept of rest, you might enjoy my doctors explanation: "It means doing nothing." NOTHING? Not meditating, not yoga? They are important too, but on top of these things, I have to find time to do nothing. Fifty years ago my doctor said she would have tucked me up in a bathchair (notwithstanding the fact I wouldn't have survived the cancer 50 years ago!). I need to give myself time and space to heal.

But, I will be honest with you. I don't want to convalesce (Footstamp, hurumph). I want to work, to use my brain, to create, to achieve, to connect. I want to fix the problems that keep me awake. I want to learn new skills, be more. Not because I don't think I'm enough. I am all good and fine as I am (well, a bit wonky. But, nobbly homegrown veg are beautiful, right?). I want all this because it courses through my veins like a narcotic. Perhaps, because I am addicted to it.

I went on some very big adventures when I was younger. I was always making plans, thinking of how to push outside my comfort zone and experience new cultures. Then, after a day in the pub and an evening singing songs, I was excitedly telling a friend of my next big adventure when she said, "You're always running away Lou. Will you ever be happy to just be at home?" She doesn't remember saying it, but it was a track-stopping moment that led to a self-promise: I wouldn't plan my next big travel until I was content to stay at home. I learned to be content at home, and then realized the damndest thing... my need to escape had dissipated. My thirst for adventure changed shape, my 'travel' became a series of explorations, not an endless run from home, and I realized that being a 'traveler' is a state of mind, not a collection of passport stamps.

I wonder now if I'm at a similar juncture. If I need to learn to be still before I can allow myself to move on again. And I wonder, if I learn to be still, what will come next? As the water stills, my reflection will crystallize. Am I ready for who I will see?

Still, girl.

Be still.

Hold, girl.

Be held.

Cry, girl.

Be free.

Live, girl.

This is life.

Louisa Trunks, 2019.

It strikes me that much of the world is in a similar place right now. This enforced Covid-19 pause-bubble, which floats on fear, lies, and death, and from which many look out on broken people and systems. Are we brave enough to learn the lessons from stillness and boredom? Are we strong enough to hold onto the good that comes from it, and use it as a stepping stone to a kinder, more conscious world? Are we ready for the realization that faster, bigger isn't always better?

But, back to me, because I'm frankly too precious about my low energy reserves to use any on world-contemplating right now. My doctor has given me 5 things to do each day: sleep, eat well, relax my mind, exercise gently, and rest.

You may have seen the new Covid-19 hot topic argument on social media: 'learn a new skill' (netflix is for dummies) vs 'this is an emergency, do what you need to survive' (give me your Netflix recommendations?) It's quite entertaining, got some good points on both sides, but generally cut from the 'you're a moron if you have a different opinion than me' twaddle that was so elegantly defined in the long forgotten Brexit era. I've got a self-satisfying solution sure to quell both sides. I'm going to master the skill of doing nothing. I think it might just be my hardest challenge yet.

-Louisa Trunks

Focus on Emotions

"...As a complementary therapist working with cancer patients, I thought I understood cancer, but nothing had prepared me for the emotional impact of a diagnosis. Since then I have taken a series of nature photographs to represent the emotional impact of cancer called 'Focus on Emotions.' This represents not only my story but also emotions and feelings that have been shared by many other cancer patients, all with different stories to tell, and my family. The images are natural, unedited other than the occasional crop and not staged. They are often everyday scenes, for example a sunrise, a sunset, flowers, beaches, and things that most of us have experienced. During a presentation, I explain a little bit about each image and why I chose it. I then let the audience have a few moments to reflect on what the image means to them.

I deliver this talk and exhibition to healthcare professionals, cancer patients, work colleagues, and the general public. I want people to understand the devastating emotional impact cancer has on lives. If people can have an insight to our emotions, I am convinced that cancer patients will have an improved quality of treatment and recovery. Cancer changes lives, but that's not always a bad thing. I now see the beauty that surrounds us all that many of us take for granted..." -Diane Leopard

*The following photographs and descriptions are from Diane's "Focus on Emotions."

Diagnosis- This picture of Dunstanburgh Castle, Northumberland represents how I felt when the consultant told me that I had breast cancer. In the foreground of this picture you can see people going about life as normal whilst my life came tumbling down.

Tears- Taken in our garden with the early morning dew after the frost had left the nasturtiums limp and lifeless. This represents the tears that I cried. Tears of sadness, confusion, uncertainty, and pain.

Tunnel of treatment- This is a beautiful, although poisonous, laburnum arch with stunning purple allium flowers standing tall and strong. The laburnum represents chemotherapy and the allium are the medical staff who care for us during treatment. The light at the end is where we all hope to be when we have gone through treatment. Taken at the Dorothy Clive Gardens.

187

Brain Fog- This represents the fog that comes over us, both as a result of treatment and the stress that a cancer diagnosis brings. Taken from my bedroom window in Endon looking towards Stanley.

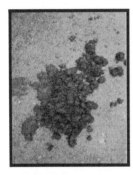

Horse muck- This needs no explanation. It is how many people tell me they feel during treatment.

End of Treatment – This empty beach represents the feeling of loneliness and emptiness that the end of treatment often brings. The sky represents a happiness that others think you should be feeling. Just like the beach, life is busy, and full, and just as the tide has gone out, treatment stops, and it can bring feelings of loneliness. Whilst some people will sadly never reach the end of treatment, this is a picture they can only dream about.

Scarred – In this photograph you can see where branches have been removed and how, over time, healing begins to take place, leaving scars both physically and emotionally. Taken at Knypersley Reservoir, Staffordshire.

New Beginnings – This is the early morning dew in our garden on the hazel tree. The delicate dew drop represents the tears we cry, and the new bud inside is the new person developing.

-All photography, descriptions, and the program "Focus on Emotions," were created by Diane Leopard

189

Undead

Color drained from flesh

Falling clumps of hair

Raining down with the shower stream.

Melting with the heat

You crawl across the cold tile

Leaving body parts behind

Until just spirit remains

Slowly floating up and into

A resting place for now.

Undead

-A commentary on chemo

by Kylee Cameron

Lines

parallel
perpendicular
zig zag

fine
read between
sign on the dotted

walk the
stay within
blurred

but the best kinds

tan lines
laugh lines
lifelines

-Kate Ellis

The Aftermath

Like their lips were sewn shut
with the silky strands of the hair
that has grown back
It all comes to a sudden halt
and the past evaporates
Transparent memories that quickly fade away
with the echoes of active treatment
Like everything that's happened over the last year
The layers of trauma, pain, and mind fuckery
have suddenly turned into warrior badges
And the metaphorical hurdles
that the fearless proudly leapt over
are worn with honor
Because it's all over
With a snap of the fingers
normal life resumes
That's what everyone thinks
but that's not how it goes down
I'm not here to spread more false truths about cancer
THIS is about the aftermath.

Nightmares have become a routine occurrence
Waking up in a cold sweat
Tears running sprints from swollen eyes
Because I've read too many stories
about this beast knocking down my door

In a few months
In a few years
And I've googled too many times
looking for honesty in a sea of pink ribbon positivity
Because I'm fucking scared to death
And so sweet dreams are no longer
but a merry-go-round of nightmarish hell
where cancer wins
and I fall off the jagged edge of a cliff
I've been climbing for the past year to my death
The only pink, the roses that surround my casket
THIS is the aftermath.

My cute figure and stylish hair have been reduced
to a map of scars and bumps and bruises
Road maps that tell of a journey
on unpaved walkways that no one wants to travel on
I hide under layers and layers
of backhanded compliments and whispers
Feeling smaller and smaller
Popping steroids to bring my body back stronger
While I work to camouflage
the tiredness that tugs at my temples
the sadness that has soured my smile
the age that fast forwarded my frown lines
There is no more looking at my mutilated self in the mirror
Because this is definitely not the girl I was supposed to be
Never thought I'd become

A disfigured anomaly
I'm not sure I can ever get used to or accept
THIS is the aftermath.

I search endlessly for signs
Fingers forever feeling their way over skin
for lump or bump or growth
That would be
Could be
Might be
Cancer cometh back.
"Feel this...Do you think it's something?"
"Can you check this? It might be..."
"There's an incessant ache. Could it have traveled..."
The obsessive unknowing and doubt
The everliving search
Will it ever end? Does it ever go away?
Or will the worry forever swim through my thoughts
and caress my butchered body?
Will I be locked in this interrogation room until my last days?
These are the questions I ask myself over and over
Everyday
THIS is the aftermath.

Met with sad eyes and sorry condolences
Doctor appointments will never be normal
Forever encountered with bad news
And Plan B's

And the shortest straw
Every. Damn. Time.
Being poked and prodded
Undressing for each and every one
Nothing is sacred
Nothing is mine alone
Breasts on display for the whole world
And all it took was a simple salutation
A curt, "Hello, I'm Doctor So-And-So,"
and he gets to see me naked
So I put on my fearless face
and whisper my mantra
"I can get through this, I will get through this,"
before every appointment
hoping for a miracle
but every one ends in the same way
Tears
Hopelessness
A deep guttural disappointment
that my body has failed me again
and when the fuck is it going to wake up?
This body of mine!
THIS is the aftermath.

-Joely A. Serino

Winter 2020

I experience the arc of getting a cancer diagnosis and then being propelled into that marathon of treatment as a side path that my life has taken, like this path exists in parallel to the rest of my life. At first I thought there would be an end to the path. I thought that eventually, life would return to somewhat normal, or perhaps a new normal.

But my experience is that the diagnosis and then the treatment that included treating the cancer that had spread, and then the infections that threatened my life, and a year of multiple surgeries, and bruising chemotherapy....

That the path cancer carved literally into my body is a path now that lives in parallel to the rest of my life: always present, always a threat, always a reminder of how my identity has been altered.

How I literally take up space and claim or not claim who I am, it's something that I now just live with and sort out each day: how I identify myself as a woman/as a mother/as a wife/as a faculty member /as a theater practitioner.

These parts of me are now interwoven to
reveal/to expose/to glorify the multiple identities
that intersect to create who I am today.

-Stephanie Burlington Daniels

How do you explain what cancer is to a child?

How do you explain what cancer is to a child? How do you explain to a three-year old that her mother's breasts are being removed? How do you stifle your child from climbing up on your lap to cuddle in your bosom after you have just undergone a bilateral mastectomy?

In "Mommy Has Boo-Boos On Her Boobies," Janice Woerner tells the story of how she empowered her daughter, Hayden, with a simple statement that became their mantra through multiple surgical procedures performed for removal and reconstruction of all her breast tissue. Janice's cancer journey began in 2010 when she was diagnosed with DCIS (Ductal Carcinoma In Situ). She was also told she would be unable to conceive a child. One year later, her daughter was conceived naturally crediting restorative yoga in helping her body heal and increasing her fertility. In 2015, the cancer had returned and Janice underwent a bilateral mastectomy. She acquired an infection in her tissue expanders that required additional reconstructive surgeries.

This story was written "as a love letter to my daughter about an explanation that I would make to give a name to what I was going through. This 'mantra' gave my daughter a way to come to terms with her mother's illness as if to think 'ok, this is a thing. My mommy has it. And everything is going to be ok.'"

My Mommy Has Boo-Boos on Her Boobies

One day my mommy went to the doctor for a checkup.
This was a special doctor that makes sure women's boobies
are healthy.

The doctor took pictures of her boobies with a special
machine.

He looked at the pictures and saw an illness in my mommy's
boobies called "cancer."

The doctor told my mommy that to make her healthy again he
would have to remove her boobies from her body.

While my mommy slept, the doctor removed my mommy's
boobies.
When he was done, my mommy had big boo-boos where the
doctor had to cut into her body to take her boobies.

This was very hard on my mommy's body. She had to stay in
the hospital for a couple of days because her body was very
weak and tired.

My mommy was so happy to see me.

My mommy told me that I would have to be very careful when
I hugged her because she had boo-boos on her boobies.

When my mommy came home, she was in so much pain. Her
boobies were very sore.

So my grandma, who I call "Wita," helped with all mommy's
chores around the house and helped take care of me.

I had to be very gentle when I would cuddle with my mommy. She would remind me to be careful because of the boo-boos on her boobies.

My mommy was so sad because she couldn't pick me up and hold me. She couldn't twirl me in her arms like she did before she had boo-boos on her boobies.

After a couple of months, my mommy was feeling better. She worked hard to get stronger, doing exercises every day.

She did lots of stretches and a special type of exercise she calls "yoga."

And soon she was able to use her arms to give me a BIG hug again!

When my mommy went back to work, she was able to help other ladies who have boo-boos on THEIR boobies.

I'm so happy that my mommy is healthy and strong again. Now we can do handstands together...

Hang from the monkey bars...

...And twirl in my mommy's arms again.

-Janice M. Woerner

Fearless

A layer of fear,

And sadness,

And hurt,

And angst

has melted away.

I am raw.

Burnt and pink,

Soft and naked,

Born again anew.

I rise from the pools of tears

that have collected within my crevices.

I lift from the depths

in which I once drowned.

I am fearless.

-Joely A. Serino

Clown

A pink ribbon

A red nose

The weight feels

Like a soggy flower

Pinned to a shirt

Squeeze the nose

Beep

Beep

Infusion complete

Laughing at the absurdity

Of this circus of sorts

Nightmarish in its humor

Shuffling along

The tingling and paint

Of the oversized shoes

May last forever

Or May stop when removed

A juggling act

Of needles

Be careful not to drop them

Or the crowd won't applaud.

-A commentary on chemo

by Kylee Cameron

Sink or Swim

People tell me:
"You're such a trouper..."
"You're a warrior...a goddess."
"You're such an inspiration."

But none of that is true.
I'm just doing
what anyone would do,
what YOU would do,
when faced with a
life or death choice,
when it's sink or swim.

I swam.

Sometimes I did the breast stroke.
Sometimes it was a frantic doggie paddle.
Sometimes I went under.
Sometimes I choked on a mouthful of water.
Sometimes I sobbed while I paddled.
But still, I kept swimming.

What choice did I have?
To give up?
That's not a choice;
that's a death sentence.

So, instead of dying,
I swam.
And I'm swimming still.

-Cathy Gigante-Brown

My heart dropped when I heard Jenicka expressed herself so openly. That night I saw my two youngest siblings in a different light. Johnny was fourteen and Jenicka was fifteen when our mom passed away. They'd lost their dad only two years earlier too on that unimaginable day they lost a parent for the second time. Then, I was determined to make sure they knew I would never abandon them. I switched into full survival mode momentarily.

My mom's trust apparently determined that the kids' guardian had to live in the house with the children. Tía Rosie had been appointed their legal guardian—a pill that was hard to swallow for me given that I had raised those kids since they came into this world—but I was still their emotional guardian. So when the kids asked me to move back to the house, I was very hesitant because I had finally begun to get used to being on my own, and I knew the situation was less than ideal. But they needed me. That's why despite the awkward custody arrangement, where I had to ask my aunt's permission for something as menial as picking them up at school, I said yes to Johnny and Jenicka determined to make it work for them. These kids were my strength—they were my heroes, and honestly, the key ingredient to my survival. While I was fighting to keep them alive, they were keeping me alive, inspiring me to stay strong, and it together and pull through no matter what.

My heart dropped,
The unimaginable day
was hard to swallow.
I was emotional, hesitant,
But I had to make it work.
I was fighting to stay strong,
to pull through no matter what.

An eerie feeling crept into the cool night.

My heart was fractured.

Every last ounce of strength, exhausted.

Mind and body slowly and mindlessly empty.

My stomach tied up in a thousand knots;

the worst possible, unimaginable life.

Surely I'd get through this crushing devastation.

I could and would handle this, but WTF?

How did I get here?

A lot of people never quite understood my desire to stay with him including some of my family—given the history I'd had with my mom before she died. But I knew that, although mishandled, it had all been to protect me and come to my defense. As a solid guy, or a gangster many many times over to be.

And when he moved any of me into the house I left anything to me without a toothbrush and he really didn't want to live in my mom's house—it just didn't feel right to me. He was determined not to let anyone think that he was taking advantage of the situation in any way. This meant that sometimes he'd head off to work early just to get ready for the day in his office, yet he always came back, night after night, to make sure we weren't alone.

"Here, take it," he'd often say, handing me a wad of cash. "I use electricity and water when I'm here with you. Please, pay for whatever you need, go buy groceries." He was an innate provider and, although the current arrangements weren't what he'd wished for, he rolled with it, giving us the space and time to heal, while also lending me the love and care I desperately needed.

As if this wasn't enough, he also stepped in and gave me a hand with Johnny. Angel would help and comfort Johnny when he crept into our room in the middle of the night scared or sad. He made Johnny feel safe and slowly became a true father figure to us both. Angel wouldn't scold him, but when Johnny was acting up or doing something that was stressing me out, Angel would step in and say,

---

I was determined to work for the space and time to heal,

the love and care I desperately needed,

and comfort in the middle of the night.

-artwork and blackout poetry by Joely A. Serino

An American Cancer Story

Spurts
of productivity
With lazy in between
Riding those waves,
Accepting
When it's enough.

Reaching out to old friends
Listening
Sometimes,
Unsurprisingly Nothing's left.

And If there were only
30 days to live
Fever, Cough,
Muscle pain, or is it loss of taste
A preemptive letter to the kids
goes viral.

Loss and
Deprived of freedom,
But engaging at home
There's much less
to maintain
than you once believed.

Take out if you can't make it yourself,
Pay it forward
a stranger
sharing the drive-thru
in pursuit of...

@ the grocery store again
1-click buying
Sweatshop $hit
Pantry and gut bursting
Are you even #content?

Caring for others
Weaker
Meeker
What's your mask
Masking
today.
It's raining
Indoors
Time spent
Spoiling loved ones
Mindful of
Double rainbows.

Serving others
vs. Servitude
Dividing the work
One love
Shake it off
bake some bread, peel an orange.*

Giving in
To your kids
Friends Parents/pets
Neighbors
Your reflection.

Drinking
more water
Juicing, tasting again
seeking stimulation
and memes,
for the sake of smiling.

Engage with the lonely
Engaged with the stressed
Panicked,
Engage
Emerge as depressed.

Tuck your kids in
being EXTRA
with kisses, conversation
A cathartic cry *or* using the cry
as a laxative.

Make your bed
in the morning
Good Luck
tonight you commingle
Shower
and the occasional bubble bath.

Duplicates
Falling off conveyor belts
Walmart, Target, Amazon
F*cking remorseless
brown boxes on your doorstep
What you want, already exists.

Reduce, Reuse, Recycle
Date nights
Birthdays
Anniversaries didn't happen
I counted
How many friends attended your quarantine drive-by.

Your kid's NBA career
On hold indefinitely.
Self-appointed celebrities
pill-popping chatter
Out of place
As one find's one's own place in the...

Week long vacations fit into a weekend
Beachfront
Hotel stay with the masses
Remorse, $$$
A social experiment
and now 14-days to reflect.

One pair of shoes
a season
moneyed or penniless
Our country burning
hand-fed by spoon or fork.

Hypersensitive to
Suffering
Misinformation and oversharing
The weeds in your garden
Truth
it's personal.

If you can't take it
anymore
Quit.

You are partly responsible
You are the party responsible
You are a responsible party.

Take responsibility.
It's the beginning
it's time to Begin
All over,
not again.

*whip your coffee

-Sky Khan

I will

Never

Ever

Ever

Ever

Ever

Ever

Be the same.

Just.

Fucking.

Face.

It.

-Joely A. Serino

Surviving cancer

is so much more

than surviving **the** cancer.

-Jillian Calahan

Butterflies and Blisters

It's a long walk, this road to recovery.
Certain it would lead me back home,
I started out with the best of intentions,
That it was a journey I could make on my own.
But it's a long walk, this road to recovery.

The path is not straight from pain to healing.
Certain my defenses would protect my soul,
I started out with my shield and my sword.
Thinking all it would take was a little control,
But the path is not straight from pain to healing.

It feels more like a mountain or being lost at sea.
When the darkness descends and there's nowhere to flee,
You can't catch your breath and fall to your knee.
Under the weight of your grief, you just want to be free...

It's in those dark lonely moments when you honour your pain,
Put down your burdens and lift your face to the rain.
When you finally acknowledge your scars and your fears,
That's when recovery begins, with those first healing tears.

This is just the start of the journey.
So put down your sword, it's no longer a fight.
The ground beneath your feet is a well-trodden path.
Take a deep breath and fill your soul with the light.
This is just the start of the journey.

It's a long walk, this road to recovery,
But I found joy on this path of butterflies and blisters.
Once I finally figured out that there's no going back,
And I'm so glad I found you, my beautiful sisters.
Because whilst it's a long walk, this road to recovery...

...We do not have to travel it alone.

-Dawn Jehle

We Had To Be

We had to be a little bit bearable

Less paranoid

With the least pessimistic approach

We had to be much strong,

More positive and most self-assured

About the blessings Almighty needs to offer you

We had to promise ourselves

To live each day of our lives wholeheartedly

With all the hopes

And try to fulfill each dream

No matter the disease

To try to subjugate the soul

We had to learn to conquer every pain

We have been dealing with

And each suffering we will face

In the journey of agony

By the slightest ray of hope

That is hidden deep inside of the core of our hearts

Like a pearl inside the oyster.

We had to be optimistic enough

To cross the vicinity of tentacles of pessimism

And reach the point

Where the soul gets strengthened enough

To embark the new journey of life

After a life threatening experience

Which we will embrace

Considering it the will of the Lord

-Mona Hemant Bakshi

Think Back to that Moment

We've all struggled.

Think back to that really bad moment.

Think back to that moment you thought you'd never get through.

That moment that you spoke to God out loud, begging to be saved, pleading to be lifted up and healed, to be freed from that devastating pain that crippled your body and haunted your mind.

That moment that you crawled into a ball, your body downright vibrating because your heart was a time bomb ready to be detonated, your soul was a pulsing shade of black, and no matter what you did or where you turned or how you positioned yourself, you couldn't be alleviated from the anguish that took over your whole being, your whole existence.

Think back to that moment that you ugly cried helpless tears, not caring what you looked like in that present time because the agony was that grueling, that severe.

That moment that you literally thought you were gonna die, felt death approaching, the reaper knocking on your door, and you were ready to be put out of your misery, ready to be taken.

If you're reading this right now, your gallant bravery and perpetual perseverance rescued your ailing body, your sickened soul, and your diminished heart.

You made it through that moment, even when you thought you'd never make it. Because when we have to, we will. And look at you now, you did it!

And so did I.

-Joely A. Serino

We Had To Be

About the Anthology Authors & Index

At the end of each author bio, you will find the page numbers where their writing or artwork can be found.

We Had To Be

K.H. Anastasia

is a Finnish author who loves romance, books, HEAs, mint tea, and writing until early morning. Her mummo (grandma) was diagnosed with breast cancer during a regular check-up in the early 2010s. Unfortunately, their story wasn't a positive one, even if they fought hard. Since then, K.H. Anastasia has donated money to breast  cancer research in many ways, including writing a letter to be included in this anthology. Her contemporary romance debut called All Your Tomorrows is available now.

*This photo is of her and her mummo. *Found on pg 168

Mona Hemant Bakshi

is the mother of three grown ups. She feels that she is motivated by her husband and her kids and that writing is a beautiful trait inherited from her late mother. She tries to encourage fellow writers and loves to read their feedback.
Follow her @meraki_by.mb.
 *Found on pg 218

Lasell Jaretzki Bartlett

Writer, Horsewoman, Somatic Therapist, Lasell (luh-SELL) writes to make sense of the impact of life events. Valuing relational safety as the foundation, she ventures into the wordless places where tangles can be unraveled and more freedom and flow become available. She is a near-death survivor (1948) and a cancer survivor (1996) who embraces grief and resilience, holding on to hope to balance the challenges of living and dying. Thanks to strong ancestors, a large circle of support, fierce determination to live, and a dollop of grace, Lasell is still here, counting the years (no longer the days and weeks and months), twenty-six years after her breast cancer diagnosis, surgeries, CMF chemo, and radiation. www.lasellbartlett.com
*Found on pg 111

Kathryn Bassett

is a 51 year old, married, teaching assistant with one 12 year old daughter. Very recently, in November 2021, after finding a lump in her right breast, she was diagnosed with Mucinous Breast Cancer, and she has had subsequent lumpectomy and sentinel node biopsy and a second re-excision op to ensure margins are clear. She is awaiting the results to understand what her next treatment plan will entail. "It's still pretty new to me, and I am using my humour and creativity to express myself and focus by keeping in the present moment." *Found on pgs 33, 88, 120

Cathy Gigante-Brown is an author and novelist who divides her time between New York (Brooklyn and Kingston) and Florida. Her works have appeared in a number of publications, including *The*

New York Times, The Huffington Post, and *Ravishly,* where she documented her breast cancer journey with dozens of essays. In April 2013 Catherine was diagnosed with Invasive Ductal Carcinoma in her left breast and underwent a mastectomy and TC chemotherapy. In October 2019 Catherine had a recurrence in her lymph nodes and had an axillary dissection, ACT chemo, and radiation. She would like to dedicate this book to her family and friends who have supported her every step of the way, especially her husband Peter and son David. Catherine is now 2 years NED and strives to live each day to the fullest traveling, cooking, writing, and practicing yoga. Cgbrownwriter.com   *Found on pgs 28, 77, 154, 204

Jillian Calahan (she/her/they) is a poet and short story writer from Seattle, Washington. In October of 2013 her aunt/best friend, Kim Johnson, was diagnosed with Metastatic Breast Cancer. Jillian quickly became her caregiver, taking her to weekly appointments, doing daily wound care/dressing changes, and staying with her in the ICU when times got tough. Through it all, Kim kept her sense of humor, always finding ways to laugh, even through

the tears and pain. Despite being told she was terminal, she fought hard to be able to stay with her children and grandbaby. They were the single most important thing in her life. Eventually her storm did pass, and Kim found her pot of gold on March 17, 2014. She is missed every single day. *The photo on the left is of Kim Johnson.

*Found on pgs 108, 165, 166, 215

Kylee Cameron

lives in Denton, Texas with her husband, cats, and dog. They also rescue and foster cats and kittens. Kylee began writing in her early school years, being published at 16. After her breast cancer diagnosis at age 30, she found writing poetry helped her process everything that comes with cancer treatment, and the creativity was reignited. She plans to continue writing as a way to bring awareness to living with chronic illness, and hopes to pursue a degree in English.
*Found on pgs 41, 85, 190, 202

Gina Carrillo, aka Black Widow

is a poet and an artist from Franklin, TN and was diagnosed with Stage 3 Breast Cancer in 2019 at the age of 34 years old. She went through a right Mastectomy and underwent radiation. She continues to do hormone treatments and is on a chemo pill for 7 more years. She had the tran flap surgery and is now cancer free! She started getting scar cover up tattoos, and they are almost complete! This anthology is dedicated to her moms, Lisa & Vickie, who were always there for her! *Found on pgs 38, 99, 156, 180

Marga (Alexandra Colta)

Born and raised in Europe, UNARTE (National University of Arts, Romania) graphic design alumna, Alexandra is an art educator and a professional artist. In appreciation for her hard work, dedication, and commitment to excellence as an art educator, Alexandra has been awarded the highest award, the Educator of the Year 2021-2022. To honor the memory of her mom's long battle with breast cancer, this piece of artwork, "One Last Anthurium," her mom's favorite flower, is dedicated to her with love. "Thank you Joely for making me a part of this unique project!" *This photo is of her mom.
*Found on pg 141

Anna Crollman

is a breast cancer survivor, infertility warrior, and self-love advocate. She is the founder of the lifestyle brand My Cancer Chic, inspiring women to thrive through adversity with self-confidence, style, and wellness. On her social media and website, she shows up as her most vulnerable and authentic self, sharing snippets of her love as a mother, entrepreneur, and style/beauty addict, inspiring you to find the joy and confidence in your own story, no matter what life throws your way.
*Found on pg 112

Stephanie Burlington Daniels

is a Professor of Theatre and Dance at Wheaton College (MA) where she teaches acting, directing, and Theatre and Social Change. Diagnosed with Invasive Ductal Carcinoma in 2017, Stephanie lived through an initial mastectomy, lymph node removal, and an infection that spread to her implant that then burst open like an exploding faucet, and required 5 corrective surgeries. Stephanie had 16 weeks of AC-T chemotherapy, and now takes Tamoxifen to decrease the chances of recurrence. Stephanie has ridden the roller coaster of survival and is now processing the experience through writing, painting, and gardening. She lives with her two incredibly strong and funny sons, Laurence and Henry; her beloved husband, Larry; and their incredible black lab, Bella.

*Found on pgs 52, 142, 196

Kate Ellis

is currently on extended leave from her job as a Kinship Worker in Child Protection. She was diagnosed at 42 with Ductal Carcinoma in situ and Stage 1B Invasive Ductal Carcinoma, ER/PR +, HER2-, with 2 unknown variants on the BRCA2 gene. She had a mastectomy and was put on Tamoxifen and Zoladex. At the age of 43, after reconstructive surgery with a prophylactic mastectomy, Kate was diagnosed a 2nd time with Ductal Carcinoma in situ, Lobular Carcinoma in situ, and Stage 1b Invasive Ductal Carcinoma. She received a Mammaprint and 4 rounds of TC chemotherapy. Kate is an avid reader, people watcher, and devourer of good shows, as well as a mom and stepmom. She lives in the Waterloo Region of ON, Canada with her spouse and two young-ish children. Follow her on IG @lump_into_lemonade.

*Found on pgs 48, 191

230

Sarah Fawcett was born and raised in Wales, and now lives in Derbyshire, UK, with her husband and two very cuddly dogs. She began writing a few years ago and has recently had pieces published in Poetic Reveries and Yours Truly magazines and The Sacred Feminine: Volume II Open Skies Anthology. If you wish to read more of her work, you can find her on Instagram under @not_just_shadow. Sarah would like to dedicate her submission to her Mum, Christine, and her God-Mother, Denise, who have both successfully been treated for breast cancer. "A huge thanks also to Joely Serino for her dedication, inspiration, and generosity in creating this wonderful book." *This photo is of her Mum and Dad. *Found on pgs 83, 136

Lori Fischer lives in North Bergen, NJ, USA. She is a widow, mother, & grandmother. She is also a clerk at JFK Elementary School & has been there for 33 years. "When I received the phone call in June 2019 informing me that I had breast cancer, all I thought about was being here with my family. From the start I knew I had to keep my thoughts & attitude positive, but of course I had my moments. I had unexpected complications with my first surgery, a double mastectomy, which led to 5 more. My recovery was more intense, painful, and a lot longer than initially expected. My twelve-year-old granddaughter insisted on staying with me. She helped me in & out of bed, drained my drains, gave me my medication, & took care of my daily needs. I will forever be thankful for her kindness, love, & unselfish gesture." Even though it was a very difficult experience, she feels blessed that she is a survivor.
*Found on pg 148

Gia Graziano resides in Bayonne, NJ, USA, and currently works as an Executive Assistant. Prior to that, she spent 15 years as an event planner for the New York Stock Exchange. In September 2021, after a routine mammogram, Gia was diagnosed with Stage II Invasive Ductal Carcinoma and is a carrier of the BRCA 2 gene. She completed 16 rounds of chemotherapy, followed by a double mastectomy with reconstruction. Writing is new for Gia, but she finds it to be beneficial to her mental and physical health. Gia is grateful for her supportive friends and family and her mother, who has been her rock since the diagnosis.
*Found on pgs 103, 158

Karin Hammler

was raised in Long Island, NY and is now a K-12 Literary Specialist in Vero Beach, Florida, USA. Her interest in art began at age 8 in an effort to emulate her older sister Birgit, who was a prolific painter. She turned her sisterly bond into art after her sister was diagnosed with breast cancer and used art to reflect her personal feelings about her sister's struggle. Art became a significant part of her grieving process. In an effort to give others the same opportunity to express their feelings through art, Karin teaches art classes called "Feel the Heal" and authored several nonfiction teaching support books, as well as a middle grade fiction book. *Found on pg 138

Laura L. Hansen is a published poet, part-time library assistant, and former independent bookstore owner. Laura lives these days where she grew up, near the Mississippi River in Central Minnesota. In the spring of 2022, Laura was diagnosed with Invasive Ductal Carcinoma and had a lumpectomy followed by a mastectomy. She has been processing this life event, as she has with other moments large and small, by writing. Single, Laura has relied on the welcomed support of her brother who has already gone through the cancer journey (and kidney disease) with his late wife Kim. Laura and Phillip's brother, Tim, passed away just a few years ago from pancreatic cancer. Neither Laura's nor Tim's cancers have been shown to have a genetic component. Due to Covid restrictions followed by her cancer diagnosis, Laura has been unable to do in-person events to promote her most recent book, The Night Journey, Stories and Poems. Laura's books can be purchased at www.riverpoethansen.com. *Found on pg 84, 146

Dawn Jehle lives in Yorkshire, UK and was diagnosed in 2018, at the age of 42, with stage 1, ER+, HER- breast cancer. She had a lumpectomy, 15 rounds of breath hold radiotherapy, and is on a 5 year course of Tamoxifen hormone therapy. She explains, "I may have lost my nipple, but I found my purpose. I started my Wonky Warriors business in honour of all women with cancer and would like to dedicate this to them. My own journey was a lonely time, which is why projects like this are so special, as we are stronger together." You can find her cancer inspired jewelry and products on her business Instagram @wonkywarriors or on her website at www.wonkywarriors.co.uk   *Found on pg 216

Sky Khan lives in Texas Hill Country with her best friend Ben and their four children. Her guiding principles have formed from time spent sitting with the dying, her study of Buddhism, estrangement from family, surviving cancer, parenting a cancer survivor, and the chaos that comes with raising four humans. Sky's projects have been mentioned twice in The New York Times. She has studied painting at The Art Students League of NY and the Austin Contemporary, as well as Interior Design principles at NY School of Interior Design. She has trained in Gestalt Psychotherapy at Gestalt Associates, Buddhism at NY Zen Center for Contemplative Care, and has a Masters in Marketing from NYU. Learn more at skykhan.com.
*Found on pgs 55, 209

Diane Leopard is a clinical complementary therapist living in Stoke-on-Trent, England - home of the pottery industry and affectionately known as 'The Potteries.' She enjoys spending time with her husband and family, and when possible, she loves getting away in their motorhome. Her hobbies include photography, writing poetry, and cycling. "At age 49 in 2013 I was diagnosed with stage 2 grade 2 mixed ductal/lobular invasive breast cancer. Treatment included surgery, radiotherapy, and hormone treatment which all went smoothly. I received excellent care from our local hospital to whom I will always be grateful. Just days after my 5 year review in March 2018, I wrote my first ever poem 'YOU' which is a reflection on my cancer journey from a devastating diagnosis to that 5 year review. Emotions were very powerful at that time and the words just seemed to flow naturally. All my poetry is influenced by personal experience but written in a style that I hope others can connect with." *Found on pgs 35, 102, 134, 186

Fiona Lochhead

is a teacher of special needs who lives in the Highlands of Scotland. In October of 2015, she was diagnosed with Triple Negative Breast Cancer at the age of 43. She underwent breast cancer surgery, six cycles of chemotherapy, and finally 19 sessions of radiotherapy, before completing treatment in June 2016. Fiona lives with her husband, children, and beloved terrier dogs. Recovery is treasured and also tough. She tries to celebrate survivorship and live fully. She makes plans for the future, fully understanding how precious it is.
*Found on pg 86

S.A. Lucero

is a paralegal by day, a bartender by night, and a mid-night writer residing in Rancho Cucamonga, CA. She has always used writing as a way to express the feelings, emotions, and situations she has found herself in. In May 2019, her Aunt Dolores (Loly) was diagnosed with Stage 3 Inflammatory Breast Cancer. Through her endless battle and tiresome body, she never gave up. Her entries in this book are dedicated to her Aunt Loly and the admiration she has for her. "I love you, Aunt Loly. On your best days (pictured here, on your wedding day) to your worst days, I'll be here for you always." *Found on pgs 50, 71, 149

Michelle Lutjen is from Port St Lucie, FL and is a stay at home mom/face painter/clown/singer in the evenings, while catching up on missed regular check ups because of lockdowns. In 2020, Michelle was faced with a breast cancer diagnosis. In the fog of fear, her wonderful family and a tribe of beautiful friends showed up. They called, they came over, they brought food and gifts, they cleaned her house, and they made her laugh. One day, bored out of her mind, she thought maybe she should tap into the artist in herself, and since she couldn't exercise her body, she should probably exercise her mind. These drawings are the result. A representation of the women in her life and the essence of them that affected her most. They are a thank you note to the beautiful women in Michelle's life. *Found on pg 150

Sally Martin lives in Chelmsford, UK with her husband, four teenage sons and two terriers. She was diagnosed in September 2017 with a Grade 3 breast cancer, which had spread to her lymph nodes. She underwent a lumpectomy, mastectomy with DIEP reconstruction, and received chemo, radiotherapy, immunotherapy, and hormone therapy. After the shock of being diagnosed with breast cancer and all the emotion that went with the territory, Sally found it therapeutic to get her "middle of the night" spiraling thoughts down on paper. Not only did poetry help her, but it also helped everyone around her to understand the emotional rollercoaster of what she was going through. Now she hopes her words will help others going through the trauma that a cancer diagnosis brings. *Found on pgs 32, 76, 118, 177

Stacy Meisel

lives in Long Beach, New York, USA and is a teacher for the visually impaired. In June 2021, at the age of 35, she was diagnosed with stage 2b Invasive Ductal Carcinoma. She went through AC-T chemotherapy, a double mastectomy with expanders, and radiation. She is currently NED and undergoing hormone therapy while waiting for her exchange surgery. Stacy would like to thank her family and friends for helping her make it through. *Found on pg 65

Amabel Mortimer

lives in Gloucestershire in the UK and is a mum to 3 teenage boys, 2 dogs, and 3 cats. She is also a lazy artist, keen gardener, and dedicated Creative Health Advocate working in the charity sector. When she was diagnosed with stage 3 Her2 and ER+ breast cancer, it was deemed aggressive but treatable. Diagnosed in 2017 at the age of 45, Amabel had 6 rounds of neoadjuvant IV chemotherapy, 22 radiotherapy sessions, lymph node removal, and a lumpectomy. Using creativity, writing and art has been a way through for Amabel, a place to contain some of the difficult thoughts and feelings around being diagnosed with breast cancer. She says it probably saved her life! *Found on pg 78

Renata Pavrey

is a nutritionist and Pilates teacher, writer, and poet. She is an Odissi dancer, marathon runner, and her hobbies and interests range from baking to knitting, gardening, reading, and trekking. Her short stories, essays, poetry, and artwork have been featured in journals, books, zines, magazines, and podcasts. She has been a contributing writer in forty-five anthologies across genres, a facilitator of two children's books, and has two solo books titled *Eunoia* and *Surrender to the Swoop*. You can find her @writerlylegacy on Twitter. She dedicates this book to her grandmother who passed away from cancer. *Found on pg 127

Angus Pratt

is a transplanted Scot who grew up in the wilds of Canada. Filling his days with volunteer work, running, writing, camping with his three boys, and rediscovering his love of watercolor painting has made life worth living and truly enjoyable. His story here is dedicated to Yvette, his wife, who died of pancreatic cancer shortly after his diagnosis. Her constant encouragement to be

"seanchaí - Gaelic storyteller" made writing easy. *Found on pg 43

Kashana D. Roman resides in
Union City, New Jersey with her mother, two
brothers, and her three dogs. Kashana, along
with her two brothers, Ricky and Gilberto,
are former students of the editor, Joely A.
Serino. Kashana's love for poetry began in
2016 when learning about blackout poetry in
Ms. Serino's 7th grade English class, and
because of her remarkable teaching,
Kashana continues to do blackout poetry to
this day and writes poems occasionally.
Kashana and her family are honored to have

met such an admirable individual and are blessed to still have her a
part of their lives. *Found on pg 164

Kristina Smith is a 40 year old wife, mother, and Previvor. Her
PALB2 gene results came back showing a mutation shortly after the
passing of her mother from TNBC in May 2021. She immediately
scheduled a mastectomy and has made it her goal through art to help
others learn about breast cancer and feel comfortable in their bodies.
*Found on pgs 54, 106, 181

Berny Stratton is 58 years old, growing up in a family with 13
siblings from Northern Ireland. She has suffered from Breast Cancer
and most recently was misdiagnosed with a benign brain tumor,
causing her to suffer from complications post-surgery. Now retired,
she was a senior Social Worker and has been married for 25 years to
her husband John, who is also now retired. To read more of her
writing, visit her Instagram page @bernycancerpoet.
*Unfortunately, right before this book was published, Berny passed
away. May her words live on forever, and may she rest in power.
*Found on pg 162

Louisa Trunks was born and raised in Somerset, the land of the Summer People, and now lives next door in Gloucestershire, UK. She is a fundraising consultant and property investor, who loves to grow and build things. Diagnosed with stage 3 breast cancer at 41, Louisa found writing a source of great comfort and established a blog as a platform for her ramblings. When not working or writing, Louisa can be found with her family, somewhere in nature, cherishing this precious life, marveling at her new post chemo curls, and giving thanks for the opportunity to see her offspring grow. She runs a lot too, because she can. Read more of Louisa's writing on her blog at https://newshinyoldfaithful.wordpress.com/
*found on pgs 30, 90, 130, 182

Vanessa Marie Upton was born in Glendale, CA., is surviving in Orange County, CA, but really wishes she lived in Disneyland on Main Street, above the Fire Station, in Walt's apartment. Vanessa is super human, her capacity to love when treated well is limitless, and she shows up for anyone in need of anything. Her three young, amazing kids and sweet family give

her more joy than anything in the world, and her friends have helped her through some really dark days. Vanessa was diagnosed with breast cancer on her 33rd birthday when she requested a mammogram as a gift, however was mocked for her young age. The women's health center changed her order for her. She thought they might have saved her life... but cancer. Her "journey" into the illness only challenged her further, quickly becoming diagnosed as triple negative metastatic after all the chemotherapy, surgeries, and radiation, concurrent with oral chemo. Cancer has taken too much from her; the devastation reigns. *Found on pg 171

Janice M. Woerner

is an Occupational Therapist, Yoga Instructor, Clinical Educator, and Inspirational Speaker based out of Central New Jersey. She is the founder and key contributor of Jersey Girl Health and Wealth, a website that provides patient education and resources for those afflicted with breast cancer and their families. She now offers workshops to help women prepare and recover from their mastectomy or lumpectomy surgeries. Contact at healthyjerseygirl@gmail.com

Janice M. Woerner, MS, OTR/L Occupational Therapist

www.jerseygirlhealthandwealth.com

*Found on pg 198

About the Cover Artist...
Jenna Philpott, MS, MFA

Jenna is a small human who will not be remembered 300 years from now, but she is grateful to be loved wildly by those who choose to love her in the now. She is an artist that is consumed with the edge, the line, and the beauty of the ordinary. She knows now that scars are ordinary. She is surprised and enchanted by maker's marks, the white space around letters, words, and punctuation. She doesn't know how to tell you about the humans and beasts and life that she loves, except to say this: she is a radical and loyal friend, a children's story collector, an appreciator of starry nights and easy days, a listener to secret dreams, and a plant lover. She is also the belly scratcher of her two Scottie dogs, and a fierce advocate for her four kids who all have dyslexia. She is proud to be the lover and friend to her husband for the last 27 years. She is a napper, a daydreamer, a maker of things, except a tidy house. She manages her woes by cracking jokes, trying new things, breathing deeply, yoga, creating whatever art suits her in the moment, and taking long walks with whomever will hold her hand. She is also a survivor of Stage 2, Grade 3, Triple Positive Invasive Ductal Carcinoma. She was diagnosed after fleeing Oregon forest fires at the beginning of the pandemic. Tell her your story, and she will tell you hers.

About the Editor...
Joely A. Serino

A middle school English Language Arts teacher in New Jersey for 20 years, Joely started writing poetry to inspire her students and never looked back. Receiving "Teacher of the Year" twice, at the age of 30 and again at the age of 40, Joely has been secretly teaching her students the art of writing poetry for years, despite it not being in the curriculum. Shhh! Don't tell anyone! She truly believes in its healing powers. In 2019, Joely wrote and self-published her debut poetry

book *This is Not the Girl I Was Supposed to Be*, which explores the ups and downs of living with a chronic illness. Her poetry has also been published in several anthologies.

In January of 2020, Joely was diagnosed with Stage 2 Invasive Ductal Carcinoma. After two surgeries, undergoing 6 months of TC chemotherapy, and 6 weeks of radiation, she is now cancer-free and working her way through survivorship while on Tamoxifen.

In her spare time, Joely loves to read, write poetry, experiment with different art forms, and spread kindness. She also enjoys eating the delicious meals her husband makes her, hanging out with a good book at the neighborhood cafe, and snuggling with her two mini dachshunds. Read more of her poetry on Instagram @beautifulmesspoetess.

Dedication...

First and foremost, to my submission authors and artists...Without all of you, this book would not have been possible. Thank you for taking a chance on a girl who had a dream. Behind every single email that you sent me was a girl in New Jersey, USA celebrating that "It's all happening!" YOU made it happen, and I will be forever grateful!

To Jenna...For your kindness and generosity and friendship, I am so grateful! From our first meeting, when you told me that, no matter what, I wouldn't have to do this alone, I knew that we were destined to be friends. You are proof that online friendships are real and true.

To my husband, Chris...Thank you for sticking by me on this cancer journey from start to finish. For all of the gourmet meals, massages when the side effects were too much, for waiting in the parking lot during every treatment and appointment, and organizing all of the moments that made me feel special, I am so grateful to have you by my side. Thank you for believing in this project, listening to all of my ideas and plans, and celebrating all of the little victories with me. I love you!

To my parents, Cheryl and Joe...Thank you for helping me get through the fight of my life with good food and lots of love. You're the best around!

To my Uncle Vin...Thank you for all of the literary advice and for believing in this project. Your texts meant more than you'll ever know. I love you!

To my team at MSKCC...Thank you for saving my life. Throughout the entire journey, all of you were there when I had a question, when I was scared, and when I needed help. You kept my family and I calm when we shouldn't have been. Thank you a million times over.

To Nicole...Thank you for always being the listening ear, the advice giver, and the cheerleader whenever I needed it. We've both been through some shit, helping each other get through all the trauma. And through it all, you've helped me to see that I am more than I give myself credit for, and I'm so grateful for that.

To Kate...When you told me that I would get the submissions needed, I don't think you realized what that simple statement did for me. You gave me the confidence to take that leap and click "post" on my Call for Submissions. Thank you for celebrating all of the small wins with me and for answering all of my stupid questions. I'm so grateful for your friendship.

To Angela...You were the first person I went to when I had the idea for this little anthology thing that I couldn't get out of my mind. Thank you for validating my ideas, believing in me, and giving me the confidence to move forward with my dream. You will forever be my "poetry coach."

To my Kennedy Family...Thank you for all of the support during my cancer journey. For the parade, all of the gifts, the messages throughout the day when I was alone during chemo, for celebrating with me when I was done with active treatment, I am so grateful to all of you that made me feel special. You prove to me over and over again that friends are the family you choose, and I would choose all of you over and over again.

To my friends at Bogota Press...Thank you for giving me a comfy place to work everyday, the best coffee around, and delicious lunches that kept me going and gave me the energy to achieve this dream. You're the best!

To the town of Bogota...For organizing the amazing parade and meal train, both while I was going through chemo, for the gifts and cards and cakes and so much love, all for a girl that you barely knew, I am so grateful to all of you. You made me feel so special and showed me that this is exactly where I belong. I will never forget how you lifted my family up during such a difficult time. Thank you a million times over! Chris and I will continue to pay it forward in any way we possibly can.

Love always,
Joely

Printed in Great Britain
by Amazon

85047302R00141